Mass Dest

Is God Guilty of Genocide?

Melvin Tinker

EP BOOKS

1st Floor Venture House, 6 Silver Court, Watchmead, Welwyn Garden City, UK, AL7 1TS

http://www.epbooks.org

admin@epbooks.org

EP Books are distributed in the USA by:

JPL Distribution

3741 Linden Avenue Southeast

Grand Rapids, MI 49548

orders@jplbooks.com

© Melvin Tinker 2017. All rights reserved. No part of this publication may be reproduced, stored in a retrieval system or transmitted, in any form, or by any means, electronic, mechanical, photocopying, recording or otherwise, without the prior permission of the publishers.

British Library Cataloguing in Publication Data available

ISBN 978-1-78397-185-5

Unless otherwise indicated, Scripture quotations in this publication are from THE HOLY BIBLE, NEW INTERNATIONAL VERSION® NIV® Copyright © 1973, 1978, 1984 by International Bible Society® Used by permission. All rights reserved worldwide.

Divinely-sanctioned murder in the Old Testament has long posed a moral dilemma for Christians. Many are quick to pass judgment on a society they do not understand, and to make false comparisons with modern atrocities, which they rightly condemn. In this timely book, Melvin Tinker brings out the many complications that are involved in reading the ancient texts, and shows that what seems alien to us was a necessary part of the divine guidance and protection given to ancient Israel. The texts will never make easy or comfortable reading, but here we have an explanation that will give us greater understanding of what transpired in the distant past and why.

Dr Gerald Bray, Research Professor, Beeson Divinity School

Today it is customary for both Christians and non-Christians to have enormous moral problems with parts of the Old Testament where God commands the Israelites to kill others. Melvin Tinker tackles these hard texts head on, showing that they cannot be dealt with in isolation from the entire narrative of the Bible and from the character of God. Set within that wider context the texts that seemed problematic make a whole lot more moral sense.

Dr Peter Williams, Warden of Tyndale House and affiliated lecturer, Cambridge University

Melvin Tinker has courageously addressed the matter of God's character and how God's goodness relates to passages in the Bible which speak of his judgement and the carrying out of his judgement by Israel. He demonstrates a profound trust in the Bible as the Word of God, a close reading of the text and commitment to seeing the parts of the Bible in the context of the whole. I have been informed and encouraged by his approach and warmly recommend his book as an excellent resource for those who wish to understand, defend and proclaim biblical truth.

Dr Peter Jensen, former Principal of Moore College and Archbishop of Sydney.

Old Testament reports of God's 'genocidal commands' have long dismayed, perplexed or troubled people inside as well as outside the churches. What we easily lose sight of is the polar depths of divine holiness and human sin. Melvin Tinker deserves our gratitude for resolutely foregrounding these truths in his treatment and informing us of the nature of the Canaanite practices in question. He invites us to orient our thought unswervingly to the being and character of God and nothing is more important than that.

Dr Stephen N Williams, Professor of Systematic Theology, Union Theological College, Belfast

For Christopher, Michael and Philip and the next generation of 'pastor-theologians'

Contents

Foreword

It is a great pleasure to be asked to write some words of introduction to the latest book of my long-time friend, Melvin Tinker. He has many gifts, one of which, not the least, is as an apologist for the faith. Melvin's contemporary style, his wide reading, his knowledge of the Bible, and his theological grasp enliven and inform all that he has to say.

The new book may be thought of as an exercise in consistency, or better, in Christian integrity. None of us have any difficulty in finding warm and comforting words from the Bible: Psalm 23, or Jesus' Sermon on the Mount, or the way Jesus welcomed children or fed the hungry and healed the sick. But the Bible has a darker side. Not only Jesus' kind words and deeds, but his anger, his driving men from the Temple with a handmade whip, his pointed remarks about the division his teaching will cause, and his statements on hell as well as on heaven, for example.

In this book Melvin is dealing with this darker side. If the Christian teaching about the Bible being one book, with one overall theme or message, is true, we must not overlook its darker side, the darker side of Jesus' ministry, but also the deeds of the 'God of the Old Testament'. In a day when the Bible is dissected by the critics, or divided by specialists, this in itself is a welcome emphasis. The Bible is the one Word of God, and its entirety is to be taken seriously and faced honestly. The darker side cannot simply be brushed under the carpet. Apart from anything else, this is simply to push the culture further away from the sunnier side of its teaching. For as was aptly said, 'If you belittle the disease you belittle the physician.' The Lord our God is one Lord. Integrity demands that we form a consistent judgement of both the shadows and the sunshine.

Preparatory to this, we need to be reminded of God's character. Any attentive reader of the Bible can see that it is impossible to make sense of it without the idea that God has a mind of his own. He is not simply the rather ineffective help to satisfying the latest desires of men and women. In any case, these are constantly shifting, with an ever-enlarging portfolio of 'rights' to benefit from. God is not a human agent, not even a human prime minister or president or business leader, but our Creator and Lord. He is not driven by his desires to please us, but is just and holy. Because of this his love, disclosed in his covenant with Abraham and in Jesus the Mediator of the Covenant, is not moody, but deep and unwavering, rooted in his own unchanging character, and involving the humiliation and death of God incarnate. God did not spare his Son but delivered him up for us all.

God has a plan. Much of the detail of this plan is hidden from us, but it is clear that it involves the choice of a people, the people of Abraham, Isaac and Jacob, and of blessing of them through a gracious covenant. This arrangement both allows for the people's chastisement if and when their fidelity to the covenant falters, and their protection from the attacks of surrounding nations intent on snuffing them out.

Paul, the Apostle to the Gentiles, says that in the Old Testament the people of God were under age, 'under guardians and managers' while being surrounded by bitter enemies. Both the correction and protection of his people required that their God undertook acts of holy discipline and destruction.

In other words, Melvin is arguing from the Bible itself, that it is necessary to contextualise the darker side of things. These are not isolated events which show us that God is capable of losing his temper, or of being vicious and bloodthirsty. This is not how the destruction of the Canaanites is to be seen. Rather they are instances of his protective care of his people, just as the disobedience of his own people has to be visited with the destructive-corrective action of God. These are parts of one consistent picture, what Melvin refers to as the non-partisan action of God. Not an isolated case of bullying or of loss of composure, but the understanding of God as 'the judge of all the earth' who 'does what is just'. Though God is high and lifted up, nonetheless he has a deep commitment of grace and love to his unprepossessing people. The nations surrounding Israel were not pure and innocent, but idolatrous and abominable. Their actions revealed their detestable character, calling for righteous punishment.

God does not suddenly grow up, as if the caterpillar of the Old Testament becomes the butterfly of the New Testament. However, his revelation does develop from being focused exclusively on Israel to his concern for the international church of Jesus Christ. This is the true, the full, 'Israel of God'. It is in Jesus Christ, the Suffering Servant, that we see God's wrath and grace best refracted.

To spell out these dark themes in some detail is characteristic of the courage and commitment to the truth that is Melvin's outlook. Some of this makes uncomfortable reading, but then Melvin's aim is not to 'speak to us smooth words ... illusions', but to be faithful to the God of Israel and the Father of our Lord Jesus Christ. As he says, both Testaments portray 'God in his holiness as implacably opposed to all sin which issues in judgement, and yet in his love he shows mercy which calls for repentance'.

Professor Paul Helm, Professor of History & Philosophy of Religion, King's College, London, 1993-2000

Preface

In an increasingly secularised Western society people may not be sure if, or what God, they believe in, but they are quite certain of the God they don't believe in: the God of the Old Testament.

There is a memorable scene in the 1980s film, *Chariots of Fire*, where two Cambridge Dons are discussing how to handle one of their students, Harold Abrahams who, against all things 'proper', 'sporting' and 'English', has hired a professional trainer to assist him in preparing for the 1924 Paris Olympics. They explain his truculence as in part due to the fact that 'he worships a different God, from a different mountain'. In other words, he was Jewish and so intrinsically at odds with the 'Christian' God. Not surprisingly, then, he had a different outlook exhibiting different behaviour and values.

Strip away the blatant racism of that statement, the underlying view it expresses still remains pervasive today, namely, that the God of the Old Testament (the God of 'another mountain'—Sinai) is decidedly not the same as the God and Father of the Lord Jesus Christ who taught a different ethic ('love your enemies') from a different hill (the Mount).

It is particularly when we come to those passages where the God of Sinai gives explicit commands to rid the 'Promised Land' of its present occupants (and such a 'getting rid' is to be by the sword, sparing neither women or children or even animals), that we ask: 'What kind of God is this who would do such a thing?' Was he 'misheard'? Did he 'misspeak'? Or was it an ancient form of 'ethnic cleansing' under the thin guise of religious calling? These and many other explanations have been given over the years.

The need to revisit some of these passages has been given a certain urgency by the rise of the New Atheists. One of the key objections raised by this group to religions in general, and Christianity in particular, is that they propagate the kind of fanaticism we see going on around the world with jihad and this is not surprising given that within the Bible itself we have what appears to be a jihad against the Canaanites. The argument goes that if such a God exists then he is 'not great', and even if he is great (i.e. powerful) he certainly is not good!

What this book seeks to do is to show that a responsible reading of these difficult passages in the light of the Bible as a whole and the fulfilment of God's purposes and promises (yes, the God of the Old Testament) in Jesus Christ, reveals they have a richer significance than may appear at first sight. They are not to be set at odds with the teaching of Jesus and other New Testament writers, for, as we shall see, very similar teaching is to be found there too. What is more, in the darkness of some of these Old Testament passages there breaks through dazzling shafts of merciful light until they all converge at the one point in history where perfect justice and perfect love meet—at the Cross of Christ.

The passages will be taken literally (which is not the same as 'literalistically') and there will be no attempt to dodge some of the penetratingly serious moral issues such as the killing of children. But neither will there be an attempt to domesticate the God who has revealed himself throughout the whole of Scripture and supremely in his Son, the Lord Jesus Christ. Let us not forget that it was he who, perhaps more than any other, spoke of God's present and future judgement using language which resembles the language of the conquest. The approach which will therefore be adopted is a 'literal-typological' one; that is, the commands will be taken as literal within their immediate historical context, but their full significance is to be found in their pointing to and preparing the way for Christ who 'fulfils all the law and the prophets' (Matthew 5:17).

I would like to thank Mark Lanier who made the writing of this book possible through his kind generosity and the use of the excellent Lanier Theological Library which is second to none. My gratitude also goes to my two colleagues, Lee McMunn and Scott McKay, for their friendship and encouragements in our discussions as 'iron sharpeneth iron'. Gratitude is also to be expressed to Philip Tinker for checking over the manuscript and giving his thoughtful comments. And, as always, my deepest appreciation goes to my wife Heather, a constant example of the 'wife of noble character' in Proverbs 31.

Soli Deo Gloria

Melvin Tinker

The Lanier Library, Houston, Texas 2016

1. God on trial

In 1949 the Christian apologist, C.S. Lewis, wrote a famous essay entitled *God in the Dock*. His concern was how to present the Christian faith to the 'ordinary modern man' in ways which would remain faithful to the Christian tradition and yet intelligible to modern hearers. In the essay, Lewis points out that one notable difference between, say, a genuine seeker after God in the seventeenth century and their twentieth-century equivalent, was that there was a degree of humility in his approach which was brought on by a sense of his own guilt before someone infinitely greater than himself. That situation, argued Lewis, had now been turned on its head:

> The ancient man approached God (or even the gods) as the accused person approaches his judge. For the modern man the roles have been reversed. He is the judge: God is in the dock. He is quite a kindly judge: if God should have a reasonable defence for being a God who permits war, poverty and disease, he is ready to listen to it. The trial may even end in God's acquittal. But the important thing is that man is on the bench and God is in the dock.[1]

Since those words were written things have moved on quite significantly. To be sure, God is still in the dock and man is firmly ensconced on the bench in his role as judge, but he is less 'kindly' towards the accused than he used to be. In fact, there is open, undisguised hostility. For example, here is Professor Richard Dawkins:

> The God of the Old Testament is arguably the most unpleasant character in all fiction: jealous and proud of it; a petty, unjust, unforgiving control-freak; a vindictive, bloodthirsty ethnic cleanser; a misogynistic, homophobic, racist, infanticidal, genocidal, filicidal, pestilential, megalomaniacal, sadomasochistic, capriciously malevolent bully.[2]

He goes on, 'the Bible's story of Joshua's destruction of Jericho and the invasion of the Promised Land in general, is morally indistinguishable from Hitler's invasion of Poland, or Saddam Hussein's massacres of the Kurds or the Marsh Arabs.'[3]

Charles Templeton echoes similar sentiments: 'The God of the Old Testament is utterly unlike the God believed in by most practicing Christians... His justice is, by modern standards, outrageous... He is biased, querulous, vindictive, and jealous of his prerogatives.'[4]

Robert Anton Wilson points to the incongruity, as he sees it, between God's commands and God's character: 'The Bible tells us to be like God, and then on page after page it describes God as a mass murderer.'[5]

In many instances the rage against God arises out of the charge being laid firmly at his door, namely, that of genocide. We are all aware that the press (and certainly the prosecution) tend to take less than a 'kid glove' approach to someone who has been accused of heinous crimes, no matter what their standing in society. And so, the thinking goes, why should God receive any special treatment? Indeed, reading the writings of some of the new atheists like Richard Dawkins and the late Christopher Hitchens, you can't help but receive the distinct impression that a fair trial is not going to be possible; the verdict has already been decided beforehand—'God is not Great'.[6]

However, we are not to think that the issue of genocide in the Bible is mere grist for the mill of the atheist, it is troublesome to many thinking Christians as well. Referring to a number of difficult Bible passages, including the 'genocide' commands of Deuteronomy 20, D. A. Carson writes:

> The truth of the matter is that most Christians (let alone non-Christians) are uncomfortable with such passages. We hear curses, and we wonder what possible place they can have in a book that tells them to turn the other cheek, to remember that vengeance belongs exclusively to the Lord, to love our enemies and to pray for those who use us shamefully. We read the passages that not only describe but mandate genocide, and we remember that when genocide takes place today there is either an international furore or perhaps a war crimes tribunal ... Some of us avoid the difficulties by passing over such passages in our Bible reading as quickly as we can. Some of us would rather 'spiritualise' all references to cursing and war, and perhaps unwittingly switch to another set of categories occupied with justice and the triumph of God. Even where such a switch is legitimate at the level of applying Scripture, we must first come to grips with the fact that real people die in Old Testament genocide ...[7]

Turning to the evidence

When we turn to God's commands to wipe out whole populations, it has to be admitted that they do seem to be unambiguous and uncompromising.

Here is a sample of the key texts:

> When the LORD your God brings you into the land where you are entering to possess it, and clears away many nations before you, the Hittites and the Girgashites and the Amorites and the Canaanites and the Perizzites and the Hivites and the Jebusites, seven nations greater and stronger than you, and when the LORD your God delivers them before you and you defeat them, *then you shall utterly destroy them*. You shall make no covenant with them and show no favour to them (Deuteronomy 7:1-2, emphasis added).

> Only in the cities of these peoples that the LORD your God is giving you as an inheritance, *you shall not leave alive anything that breathes. But you shall utterly destroy them*, the Hittite and the Amorite, the Canaanite and the Perizzite, the Hivite and the Jebusite, as the LORD your God has commanded you (Deuteronomy 20:16-17, emphasis added).

The biblical narrative suggests that the commands were taken seriously and quite literally:

> They [Israel] utterly destroyed everything in the city [Jericho], both man and woman, young and old, and ox and sheep and donkey, with the edge of the sword (Joshua 6:21).

If genocide is to be defined as 'the deliberate killing of a large group of people especially those of a nation or particular ethnic group' (Oxford Dictionary) then prima facie there appears to be a case to answer. God's position in the dock seems to be justified and the charge is serious—mass murder!

No case to answer?

Before mounting a case for the defence it may be worth noting two responses to these Old Testament texts which, if accepted, would mean there is in fact no case to answer.

1. The genocide took place but the Israelites were mistaken in thinking that God had commanded them. This is the position taken by Peter Enns:

> My own approach is simply to acknowledge that the Israelites were an ancient tribal people and thought of God the way other ancient tribal peoples did—as a fierce warrior who goes to battle with his people, assured of victory if they are on good terms with the deity but suffering defeat if not. This biblical portrait of God is already critiqued to a certain extent in Israel's own writings (e.g. the book of Jonah) and is put to rest in the gospel, where Jesus says we don't kill people to take their land anymore.[8]

Paul Coulter, whilst not agreeing with this position, points out that this argument is based on the premise that the mass killings were a carry over from a pagan way of understanding God: 'It was not uncommon for kings in the Near East of Old Testament times to annihilate the populations of whole cities as an offering to their gods. For example, the ninth century BC Moabite Stone records King Mesha's boast that he had destroyed all the inhabitants of Astaroth as a sacrifice to his god. The suggestion is made that Israel at the time of Joshua had a limited understanding of God and that they wrongly thought that their God, Yahweh, expected the same kind of sacrifice.' The problem, as Coulter goes on to point out, is that, 'This line of reasoning raises serious questions about the nature of God, in particular whether or not He is able to make Himself clearly understood and whether or not He would allow such blatant disobedience to go unchallenged.'[9]

A similar position to that of Enns is adopted by C.S. Cowles: 'Canaanite genocide was executed by fallible and sinful Israelites just as prone to idolatry, disobedience, and wickedness as the people they destroyed.'[10] Cowles attempts to get God off the hook by appealing to progressive human understanding of God: 'The problem of partial or even distorted concepts of God in the Old Testament has never been on God's side but on the side of the human mediators of that revelation ... As they received more light, their view of God correspondingly changed.' But as well as this creating a whole host of other problems, not least that the God of the Old Testament is seen to be decidedly different from the God of the New Testament (which seems to be a nod in the direction of a heresy called Marcionism)[11], the objections raised by Coulter against Enns applies in this case too, God is either incapable of communicating clearly, or unable, or unwilling to allow such behaviour to go unchecked.

2. We have misread the texts and failed to take into account the nature of the genre and its use of hyperbole.

Paul Copan has argued that taking these commands entirely at face value would be to misread the literature. To be sure God gave the directives, (the Israelites hadn't thought these up on their own) but, so runs the argument, we must accurately understand God's intention before we can accurately assess God's commands. Copan draws attention to the fact that writings of this period commonly traded in hyperbole (exaggeration for the sake of emphasis) especially when it came to military conquest. 'Joshua's conventional warfare rhetoric,' Copan writes, 'was common in many other ancient Near Eastern military accounts in the second and first millennia BC.'[12] 'Phrases like "utterly destroy" or "put to death men and women, children, and infants"—and other "obliteration language"—were stock "stereotypical" idioms used even when women or children were not present. They did not indicate complete annihilation.'[13]

Copan also views the main purpose of the conquest to be expulsion (driving out the inhabitants) and cleansing the land of idolatry by destroying every vestige of the evil Canaanite religion, rather than the complete annihilation of the inhabitants per se. 'You shall tear down their altars, and smash their sacred pillars, and hew down their Asherim, and burn their graven images with fire' (Deuteronomy 7:5). This was a process which would be gradual, taking place over a period of time: 'The LORD your God will clear away these nations before you little by little. You will not be able to put an end to them quickly, for the wild beasts would grow too numerous for you' (Deuteronomy 7:22).[14]

There is much in what Copan writes which is to be commended. A responsible reading of the Bible requires that genre is respected (for example, proverbs are not to be read as case law). A study of parallels with contemporary documents can yield valuable insights. It certainly appears that expulsion rather than wholesale killing was one of God's main purposes in the conquest of Canaan; after all, the

Israelites were not told to pursue the Canaanites. If this is so, then the charge of 'pure' genocide somewhat diminishes.

However, it is admitted by Copan that Joshua in leading the invading Israelite army did take the commands seriously (literally?) as evidenced by Joshua 10:40:

> So Joshua subdued the whole region, including the hill country, the Negev, the western foothills and the mountain slopes, together with all their kings. He left no survivors. He totally destroyed all who breathed, just as the LORD, the God of Israel, had commanded.

While we may allow for some degree of exaggeration in recounting some of the victories, the commands do not lend themselves all that well to this kind of interpretation. What is more, idolatry is not some abstract idea; it is generated by particular people and so it could be argued that to make certain (as is humanly possible) that the practice is going to be permanently stopped, then the only way that could happen would be by getting rid of the practitioners entirely. And so Clay Jones writes:

> Idolatry is not some mere individualistic, private hobby that a person does (for example, 'he committed the sin of idolatry'). To the contrary, it can form an entire group identity and way of life because those who commit idolatry do so as a result of being idolatrous. Idolatry is a form of worship because it involves ascribing attention and affection to something considered being worthy. Worship, regardless of its object, is inescapably whole life formational.[15]

Of course, it has to be shown that at the very least such a course of action is morally justified as well as being practically necessary.

At this point it might be worth pausing to heed this salutary warning of D. A. Carson:

> However hard some things are to understand, it is never helpful to start picking and choosing biblical truths we find congenial, as if the Bible is an open-shelved supermarket where we are at perfect liberty to choose only the chocolate bars. For the Christian, it is God's Word, and it is not negotiable. What answers we find may not be exhaustive, but they give us the God who is there, and who gives us some measure of comfort and assurance. The alternative is a god we manufacture, and who provides no comfort at all. Whatever comfort we feel is self-delusion, and it will be stripped away at the end when we give an account to the God who has spoken to us, not only in Scripture, but supremely in his Son Jesus Christ.[16]

This warning is to be linked with a challenge made a number of years ago by the Old Testament scholar, John Bright:

> I find it most interesting, and not a little odd, that although the Old Testament on occasions offends our Christian feelings, it did not apparently offend Christ's 'Christian feelings'! Could it really be that we are ethically and religiously more sensitive than He? Or is it perhaps that we do not view the Old Testament —and its God—as He did?[17]

It is important that we do justice to all the relevant biblical data as much as possible and not engage in a 'pick and choose' approach. It is also vital to seek to follow Christ's own example in viewing the Old Testament Scriptures as Jesus did, as being divinely inspired and authoritative and the final arbiter in matters of belief and practice (Matthew

19:4), with that same Old Testament Scriptures preparing the way for his own coming (Luke 24:44-48). Accordingly, all the commands and narratives concerning the eradication of the Canaanites will be taken at face value and then an attempt will be made to understand their meaning and draw out their significance in the light of Scripture as a whole and especially their fulfilment in Jesus Christ.

In brief, I hope to show that the charge of genocide is wholly unwarranted and the comparisons made by Dawkins between God and Hitler and Saddam Hussein are seriously wide of the mark. The argument made will be cumulative and multifaceted, showing that what is depicted as occurring in the conquest narratives is more finely nuanced than crude charges of 'genocide' allow. What is more, I hope to show that in the light of the New Testament's fuller revelation of God in the person and work of Jesus Christ, the Canaanite conquest takes on a much richer and far deeper significance for us today than many people might think.

2. Laying the groundwork

How do you answer the question: 'Have you stopped beating your wife?' It is not all that easy when you think about it. Part of the problem is that we feel we have been painted into a corner simply by the way the question has been framed. If you were to reply, 'I haven't stopped beating my wife' (because you never started beating her in the first place) you will appear a bully. If you say, 'I have stopped beating my wife', then that implies you had been engaging in domestic violence for some time. It feels a bit like this when we come to consider the objections raised regarding what appears to be God's commands to Israel to engage in acts of genocide. The defence appears to be on the back foot simply because the objectors are selective in what they will and will not admit as evidence. Rather, in the interests of fairness, the commands and related narratives should be considered on their own terms.

For this to be so, two important considerations need to be taken into account.

Worldviews

Peter J. Williams argues that one of the major causes of contention between the New Atheists and Christians in dealing with these controversial texts is the differing worldviews (*Weltanschauung*) held.[18]

We all have a set of presuppositions and background beliefs by which we view life.[19] These act like a pair of spectacles which we put on in the hope that we will see the world clearly so that we can navigate our way through life with significance and meaning. As Professor David Wolfe puts it, belief systems are projects which are concerned with 'making sense out of total experience.'[20]

By definition, the atheist lives in a 'world without windows', to use the term coined by Peter Berger. For the atheist there is no God who gave commands to the Israelites and no miracles which might have provided warrants for them to obey those commands. This places the atheist in an interesting position. On the one hand he expresses outrage that God could give commands of genocide, and on the other denies the existence of such a God who, therefore, could not have given such commands! As a result, the commands have not only to be explained, but explained away on purely naturalistic grounds (e.g. a people seeking theological justification for what was essentially nationalistic aggression, hence the comparison with Hitler). After all, what other possible explanation could there be since God does not (or probably does not) exist?

Many of the arguments of the New Atheists are *ad hominem*[21] and could easily be turned back on themselves by pointing out that the great genocides of modern times have been committed by those who adopted a distinctively atheistic outlook, thus switching the 'see what religion leads to' argument into 'see what atheism leads to'!

In many ways the twentieth century could rightly be claimed to have been the atheist's century. This is the period Alexander Solzhenitsyn dubbed 'the cave man century'. It was that arch-atheist Joseph Stalin who said, 'A single death is a tragedy, a million deaths is a statistic' and he should have known because under him over 40 million of his fellow countrymen were wiped out. Between 1914 and 1990 the population of the world tripled, 'but' writes Philip Bobbit, 'an estimated 187 million persons—about ten percent of the population of 1900—were killed or fated to die by human agency'.[22]

Furthermore, the stance being adopted is rather unfair because it rules out of court on a priori grounds arguments a Christian would wish to draw upon to explain the meaning and significance of the commands. This would include the belief that they were given by God who has a certain character and has supernaturally revealed his intended good purposes which are substantiated by miraculous events.

Respect the whole narrative

In turning to any literature it is vital for a correct reading and interpretation to acknowledge both the genre (type of literature) and the context. Both mischief and misunderstanding result if statements are wrested out of context and then placed within an entirely different setting. For example, there is the true story of a former Archbishop of Canterbury (Dr Michael Ramsey) who, on arriving in New York, was asked by a newspaper reporter whether he would be visiting a nightclub while in town; to which the

Archbishop innocently responded, 'Are there nightclubs in New York?' (He was rather heavenly-minded even for an Archbishop!) The following day the headline appeared in the local newspapers: 'Archbishop asks: "Are there nightclubs in New York?"'! Something similar can happen with the commands regarding the killing of the Canaanites. Stripped out of context and then recast within the framework of twenty-first-century values and assumptions the commands do appear stark, brutal and barbarous as they are made to 'stand alone'.

This is precisely what C. S. Cowles does to great effect in his book. Cowles begins his treatment by juxtaposing an account of the Canaanite killings alongside the genocide in Rwanda, thus 'softening up' the reader to accept his case for 'radical discontinuity' as if the two events were the same. The idea being that since we are rightly appalled at the one (the massacre of the Tutsis) we will equally be appalled by the 'massacre' of the Canaanites as if there were no significant differences between the two events. He then throws in a few references to the Crusades and European religious wars for good measure so ensuring that the softening up process is complete.[23]

But, as we shall see, the commands don't 'stand alone' and are part of a bigger picture.

P. J. Williams convincingly argues that the whole narrative setting (the commands and the ensuing conquering stories in the book of Joshua) should be respected and carefully attended to.[24] The commands and explanations appear within the context of a broader narrative regarding God's revealed character, his relationship to his creation as its Ruler, the redemption of his people as their Saviour and his ultimate purposes for the world as

Rescuer and Judge. To strip out the commands to conquer the land does violence to this narrative and distorts the nature of the commands so making them malleable to alternative, subjective polemical interpretations.

The importance of paying close attention to the canonical context of Joshua is important for another reason as argued by S. N. Williams, 'We are meant to read Joshua in its canonical context, where we have already learned divine grief on account of human violence; already learned of divine accommodation to human ways; where we shall learn of God's care for lilies and sparrows; where we shall learn that he will establish, for his own delight, shalom. The upshot is surely this: we must say that if God commanded the slaughter of the Canaanites, it was with an immeasurably heavy heart.'[25]

Follow the Bible's plot line

It is the larger big picture (or metanarrative) which helps us make sense of the nature and intention of the commands themselves as they relate to the character of God, the nature of his covenantal promises and his redemptive purposes culminating in the life, death and resurrection of Jesus Christ. Thus, the commands and events have to be placed along the 'plot line' of the Bible's story to see how they properly relate not only to the conquest events but to their fulfilment in Jesus Christ. This is the most biblically faithful and hermeneutically productive approach which is very much in line with the way Jesus saw his person and ministry in relation to the whole of Scripture:

> I submit that it was because Jesus saw himself as
> fully part of the same story of what happens

> when holy love meets unholy rejection, or when the Creator-Redeemer engages the forces of chaos. Stated differently: Jesus reads the Old Testament not literalistically (as do some of his critics) but in a literal-typological manner that keeps the overarching plot (that is, salvation history) in view at all times.[26]

The basic outline of the biblical story is that the sovereign and wholly good God created a good universe. We human beings rebelled and that rebellion is now such a part of our existence that we are totally enmeshed in it. All suffering (including suffering caused by war) which we now experience turns on this fact, and is in some way related to 'sin' (but not all suffering is related to sin in the same way).

The Bible centres on how God takes action to reverse these terrible effects by dealing with their root cause—sin itself. Furthermore, the Christian believer sees on the broader canvas the future dimension of a new heaven and earth where sin and sorrow will be removed, never to be experienced again.[27] This means that there is a fundamental recognition by the Christian that the world in which we live is thrown out of joint at every conceivable level—it is not the 'best of all possible worlds'. The price of sin is great, and suffering in this life is in some measure a consequence of it. Perhaps the cry of our post-Enlightenment generation echoing the cry of a man like Voltaire is, 'How can God be so cruel?', whereas the cry of earlier generations was one with a man like Martin Luther, namely, 'How can God be so merciful?' The reason why we find it difficult to say the latter (but not the former) is because we fail to appreciate the seriousness of sin and the pure character of a God who stands over and against it.

This opens up for us an important element in the discussion which is often overlooked by modern-day opponents of Christianity, namely, how God's righteous anger is to be construed in such a way that it perfectly relates to his love in bringing about his good purposes in the world. As we shall see, part of those good purposes is the destruction of evil itself. This aspect of the 'sinfulness of sin' and God's implacable opposition to it is very important in helping us move to a deeper understanding of this part of the Old Testament narrative.

Given the corrupting nature of sin in the world and God's unflinching opposition to it by virtue of his holiness, Daniel Gard is surely correct when he writes:

> A more pertinent question than why God commanded such brutal practices as the extermination of the Canaanites is why he did not command the destruction of the entire human race in time and history. He once did so at the time of Noah, but even then he preserved a remnant in the ark. He used human armies against his own people in 'reverse holy war' but always preserved a remnant. The question is truly not one about God's love but about his justice, once acted out in history as it will be on the last day. He preserved then and will always preserve his own people.[28]

But this raises questions concerning the nature of God's love, his justice and how they relate to each other, questions which will be explored in a later chapter.

3. Character and commands

There are two important considerations to take into account when someone is being accused of acting in an immoral fashion.

Character counts

The first is the question of their character. Is what is being claimed consistent with their known character or is what is known of their character at odds with the charge being made against them such that it at least raises the possibility that what they are being accused of is being wrongly construed?

The second is to consider the nature and the purpose of the acts or commands to see if they really are as 'immoral' as is being claimed.

Let's take the question of God's character first.

To some degree, whether or not we should obey someone, is not solely a matter of whether we think at first sight a command is moral or immoral. It certainly is a consideration, but not the only one. Whether we should obey a directive is also dependent upon the one who is issuing it. This is not simply a matter of someone having authority to issue commands per se otherwise the defence used by many Nazis at the Nuremberg trials would have held —'I was only obeying orders'. However, in the case of God, unlike human authorities, he not only has a right to issue commands because he is the ultimate authority (there is no higher authority to which to appeal), but the commands he gives are underwritten, as it were, by his character—the type of God he is. Scripture portrays God as holy, just, good and true, who will bring about his good and perfect will in his world.[29] To be sure, this is part of what creates the tension for the believer, understanding how a good God could issue commands which *prima facie* appear immoral—the killing of men, women and children. But it may be that a clearer understanding of God's character sheds light on the nature of the commandments in such a way that they can be (and perhaps should be) understood differently.[30]

According to the biblical narrative, Israel had reasons to obey God's commands for they had good grounds to trust God. This trust was based upon his revealed character. To use a more philosophical term, they had substantial epistemological warrants for carrying out such imperatives.[31] According to the biblical passages we are not talking about some individuals in the leadership of Israel claiming to have heard 'inner voices' to commit mass murder (the stuff of psychotics), with the rest of the people blindingly going along with them. The whole Old Testament narrative up to this point gradually and unambiguously reveals the character of God as he appeared to Abraham and the Patriarchs. God is shown as one who relates to people covenantally with an ultimate desire to bless all the nations (Genesis 12:2-3; 22:18) and who makes promises and keeps them (Genesis 15, 17, 22). He is portrayed as someone who reveals himself clearly and personally (Genesis 18; Exodus 3). He is a righteous God who abhors wickedness and responds to it in judgement (Genesis 19) and who will not act unjustly (Genesis 18:25). Furthermore, he is a God who is patient and longsuffering —'In the fourth generation your descendants will come back here, for the sin of the Amorites has not yet reached its full measure' Genesis 15:16—a key text as we shall see. He shows himself to be one who shows compassion to his people and acts in history with great displays of miraculous signs and wonders (Exodus). Finally, God reveals his holy character and his commitment to the well-being of his people by means of covenant and law (Exodus 20; Leviticus). The character of Yahweh is displayed through the narrative in what he says and does which, when taken together, would mean the people of Israel would have every good reason to obey his commands, even though at face value some may appear to be 'questionable' by our modern day standards (as for example the command to Abraham to sacrifice Isaac in Genesis 22).

So what are the 'immutable non-negotiables'[32] with regards to the character of God that we find in the Old Testament narrative which frames both the nature and purpose of the commandments to remove the Canaanites from the land, as well as giving the Israelites epistemological warrant to do so?

There are two fundamental categories by which the God of Israel is to be identified.[33]

Gracious holiness

God is revealed and so known by his special name Yahweh (Exodus 3:14ff). It is the personal covenant name which not only declares God's self-existence (what theologians call God's aseity), but the willingness to draw upon his capacities for the well-being of his people, such that Yahweh may not only be rightly rendered 'I AM' but 'I-will-be-whatever-I-need-to be'[34] for the sake of his people. In addition to the name, God's identity and character are known through his acts in history. He is portrayed as the one who brought Israel out from Egypt accompanied by remarkable events to create a people special to himself (Exodus 20:2; Deuteronomy 4:32-39; Isaiah 43:15-17). What is more, there have been verbal revelations of his character, most significantly given to Moses in Exodus 34:6-7, 'Yahweh, Yahweh, a God merciful and gracious, slow to anger and abounding in steadfast love and faithfulness, maintaining love to thousands and forgiving wickedness, rebellion and sin. Yet he does not leave the guilty unpunished; he punishes the children and their children for the sin of the fathers to the third and fourth generation.' As Richard Bauckham remarks:

> The acts of God and the character description of God combine to indicate a consistent identity of the one who graciously acts towards his people and can be expected to do so. Through the consistency of his acts and character, the one called YHWH shows himself to be one and the same.[35]

The graciousness and mercy of God, as well as his faithful love (*hesed*), are fundamental to who he is and how he relates to his creatures.

But there is also the holiness of God which is expressed in his wrath towards those who sin in rebellion against him. This is as much part of this 'credo' as the elements of grace and needs especially to be borne in mind in our present discussion.[36] As R. C. Sproul rightly observes:

> The holiness of God is at the heart of the issue
> of the conquest of Canaan. It was because of His
> holiness that the act was ordained. On the one
> hand He moved to punish the insult to His
> holiness that was daily perpetrated by the
> Canaanites. On the other hand He was
> preparing a land and a nation for a holy
> purpose.[37]

This, however, needs to be set alongside S. N. Williams' call to recognise divine accommodation in the way God acts signalling the heaviest of hearts with which any such commands would have been given (perhaps Jesus' response to Jerusalem in Luke 13:34 is the incarnational expression of such a heart? (See chapter 9)).[38]

God rules

The second important category by which the God of Israel is to be identified is that of Creator and sovereign ruler of all things. The opening chapter of Genesis establishes this and is a recurrent theme throughout Scripture (e.g. Psalm 104; Job 38-41; Isaiah 44:24). In Isaiah 40-55 both themes are developed with reference to the future—the eschatological fulfilment of God's promises of a new Exodus, and the display of his sovereignty which will be recognised by all the nations (especially Isaiah 45:22-23) such that Yahweh alone is seen to be God. In short, the Creator-Redeemer Yahweh is supreme over all things.

All of this is important for a number of reasons.

First, it is the revealed identity and character of God which provide the primary theological framework within which all his commandments and actions are to be placed. The commands don't 'stand alone'. It is in the light of the fundamental 'immutable non-negotiables' of God's character such as his holiness, righteousness, faithfulness, and grace that we are to seek to understand the commandments to remove the Canaanites from the land. Could it not be that far from the commands bringing God's righteousness into question, they actually express it at this particular juncture in salvation history? How they might do that we shall look at in a moment. The important point being made here is that the controlling concepts for all our thinking are the revealed attributes and character of God.[39]

Secondly, it is the revealed identity of God which provides sufficient warrants for God's people to obey these commands. In the first instance we may not be able to see how such commands are to be squared with the revelation that Yahweh is slow to anger and merciful. But it may be less difficult to see how they square with his revelation that he is a holy God who will punish sin extending to subsequent generations (Exodus 34:7). The wisdom required on our part as readers is to discern which aspect of God's character and purposes are being displayed at which particular points in the narrative.

Thirdly, God as Sovereign Creator-Redeemer whose very being defines what is good, at least implies that *he* has morally sufficient reasons for destroying the Canaanites. If this is so, then the means he chooses to implement them are to some degree incidental. If day by day, 'the Lord gives and the Lord takes away' and if there are instances when this 'taking away' is explicitly a matter of judgement, then he has a right to command Israel to be his servant wielding the sword in wrath (c.f. Romans 13:4, where civil authorities are described as 'God's agents for wrath'). Greg Koukl makes this point well when he writes:

Making life and taking life are the appropriate prerogatives of God. He has privileges that we do not. Though we shouldn't play God, certainly God can play God, so to speak. Just as the owner has latitude the hired hand does not, the Creator has freedoms creatures do not share. ... This is part of what we mean when we say God is 'sovereign'. The Maker has complete authority over what He has made—not simply in virtue of His power (omnipotence), but in virtue of His rightful ownership. Everything God created is His. He can do as He likes with anything that belongs to Him—which is everything ... Appealing to the sovereignty of God is not meant to silence opposition with a power move (How dare you question God he is bigger than you?!). Rather, it's meant to put the issue into its proper perspective. God has full and appropriate authority when it comes to issues of life and death. Being the Author of life, He has the absolute right to give life or to take life away whenever He wishes.[40]

Reasons to trust and obey

The business of trusting someone enough to do what they require even when we are sometimes in the dark can be a subtle business. We don't always have to have complete, cast iron guarantees before we exercise that kind of faith. This point is well illustrated by the famous parable of 'The Stranger' by Professor Basil Mitchell:

In time of war in an occupied country, a member of the resistance meets one night a Stranger who deeply impresses him ... The partisan is utterly convinced at that meeting of the Stranger's sincerity and constancy and undertakes to trust him. They never meet in conditions of intimacy again. But sometimes the Stranger is seen helping members of the resistance, and the partisan is grateful and says to his friends, 'He is on our side.' Sometimes he is seen in the uniform of the police handling over patriots to the occupying power. On these occasions his friends murmur against him: but the partisan still says, 'He is on our side.' He still believes that, in spite of appearances, the Stranger did not deceive him ... Sometimes his friends, in exasperation, say, 'Well, what would he have to do for you to admit that you were wrong and that he is not on our side?' But the partisan refuses to answer. He will not consent to put the Stranger to the test.

Mitchell goes on, 'The partisan in the parable does not allow anything to count decisively against the proposition, "the Stranger is on our side". This is because he is committed to trust in the Stranger. But he of course recognises that the Stranger's ambiguous behaviour does count against what he believes about him. It is precisely this situation which constitutes the trial of his faith'.[41]

The relevance of this story for our discussion of the Canaanite genocide is that Yahweh is far from a 'Stranger'. If the partisan in the parable had (in his own mind at least) sufficient warrants for trusting the 'Stranger' despite some ambiguous behaviour which for others might count against such trust, how much more on the basis of God's self-revelation did the Israelites have good reasons for trusting Yahweh which led them to obeying all that he commanded at this point in their history?

Before moving on to consider the nature and purpose of the commands and subsequent action by the Israelites, we need to explore the relation between God's holiness (and how that is expressed towards sin and rebellion in wrath) and his love.

4. Wrath versus love

That Yahweh expresses his wrath is not in doubt. There are over 600 references to God's wrath in the Old Testament in addition to other terms which signify the same thing, for example, when God is spoken of as being a 'jealous God' (Exodus 20:5; 34:14). This wrath is not partisan. There are many references to times when such wrath in the severest terms is said to be displayed against God's own people, Israel, as illustrated by this passage from the prophet Ezekiel:

> Therefore as surely as I live, declares the Sovereign LORD, because you have defiled my sanctuary with all your vile images and detestable practices, I myself will withdraw my favour; I will not look on you with pity or spare you. A third of your people will die of the plague or perish by famine inside you; a third will fall by the sword outside your walls; and a third I will scatter to the winds and pursue with drawn sword.
> Then my anger will cease and my wrath against them will subside, and I will be avenged. And when I have spent my wrath upon them, they will know that I the LORD have spoken in my zeal.

> I will make you a ruin and a reproach among the nations around you, in the sight of all who pass by. You will be a reproach and a taunt, a warning and an object of horror to the nations around you when I inflict punishment on you in anger and in wrath and with stinging rebuke. I the Lord have spoken. When I shoot at you with my deadly and destructive arrows of famine, I will shoot to destroy you. I will bring more and more famine upon you and cut off your supply of food. I will send famine and wild beasts against you, and they will leave you childless. Plague and bloodshed will sweep through you, and I will bring the sword against you. I the LORD have spoken. (Ezekiel 5:11-17)

The non-partisan nature of God towards the kind of evils being perpetrated by the Canaanites is also reflected in Deuteronomy 13:12ff where those in Israel who are found guilty of the same kind of practices are threatened with the same judicial consequences:

> If you hear it said about one of the towns the LORD your God is giving you to live in that troublemakers have arisen among you and have led the people of their town astray, saying, 'Let us go and worship other gods' (gods you have not known), then you must inquire, probe and investigate it thoroughly. And if it is true and it has been proved that this detestable thing has been done among you, you must certainly put to the sword all who live in that town. You must destroy it completely, both its people and its livestock. You are to gather all the plunder of the town into the middle of the public square and completely burn the town and all its plunder as a whole burnt offering to the LORD your God.

The immediate problem we face is that we tend to equate such biblical references to divine 'wrath' and 'jealousy' with similar human reactions. Whilst bearing in mind that Scripture is drawing upon language used in the human sphere, it does not mean that such transference can take place without qualification. There is a profound sense in which God's wrath is not like ours.

Sometimes human wrath is simply the result of having a quick temper which may result in a hasty and disproportionate reaction to something which is wholly unjustified. Perhaps someone makes what they think is a gentle critical comment to a friend, only to find themselves getting a good dressing down for their troubles. Is there any evidence that God is like that? Richard Dawkins clearly thinks so, which is why he calls God a 'malevolent bully'.

The evidence is actually in the opposite direction. What comes over time and time again is how incredibly patient God is with people who do the most appalling things. God's wrath is far removed from such human traits in that his wrath is the chosen, measured, proper response to that which is sinful and stands against him in his holiness.

Similarly, when we speak of someone being 'jealous', for us this is a vice, the 'green eyed monster' which is often a reaction arising out of a feeling of inadequacy as we become envious of someone who has something we do not have. Since God is completely sufficient within his own being, then he obviously could never be jealous in this sense since he lacks nothing. Therefore, God's jealousy must be something quite different to ours.

However, there must be some similarity and overlap between what human beings experience as wrath and jealousy and those qualities of God represented by these terms; otherwise they would serve no purpose in helping us know what God is like.[42]

A moment's reflection will show this to be so. Take, for example, the situation when a major world government which has the power (and in the sight of others such as the United Nations) the authority and ability to act, sees an appalling humanitarian situation developing in another country. The leaders of that government might well express their 'righteous indignation' by way of political communiqués, trade sanctions and the like. In certain cases they could be said to be expressing their 'wrath' by means of proportionate military action.

Similarly, with the notion of 'jealousy'. When a husband seeks to protect a love-relationship or avenge it when it is broken, far from this being a vice such a posture could be viewed as a virtue.[43] Such 'jealous' protective action can be taken as a sign of love. What would we think of a husband who said that he loved his wife, and yet after her having got caught up in an adulterous affair, simply remarked with a shrug of the shoulders 'That's life, these things happen, never mind'? At the very least we would question his claim that he loved her. Such love shows itself not by indifference but by 'jealousy'. Therefore, if human beings rightly respond to evils in this way, how much more should God who does not have the imperfections which often distort our reactions?

Getting personal

It also needs to be said that in God's measured response to wickedness by his wrath, there is a distinct emotive element. That is to say, God's wrath is personal. This was something which was contested many years ago by Professor C. H. Dodd and has had a profound influence upon the church's thinking in the West ever since.[44]

He argued that such ideas were both archaic and primitive. Instead, he reasoned, what is often thought of as 'God's wrath' is simply the impersonal outworkings of human beings going against the moral grain of the universe. Just as the law of gravity will have its inviolable effect upon a person if they jump off the top of a tall building, so, it is argued, human beings will suffer if they adopt attitudes and actions which go against the moral law woven into the fabric of the world.

Dr Leon Morris convincingly demonstrated this view of God's wrath to be wholly inadequate and at variance with the overwhelming testimony of Scripture where God's anger is portrayed in deeply personal terms.[45]

However, unlike his love, God's wrath is a 'secondary attribute'; it is not intrinsic to his being. Thus one can say that 'God is love' (1 John 4:8) in a way one cannot say 'God is wrath'. God's wrath is his holiness provoked externally. God's love is his steadfast 'other-person centeredness' eternally generated within the Triune Godhead. To use Martin Luther's phrase, God's wrath is his 'strange work'.[46]

The necessity of wrath being an expression of God's goodness and love has been clearly put by Croatian theologian Miroslav Volf. His reflections are made against the backdrop of genuine genocide he and many others experienced in former Yugoslavia:

> I used to think that wrath was unworthy of God. Isn't God love? Shouldn't divine love be beyond wrath? God is love, and God loves every person and every creature. That's exactly why God is

wrathful against some of them. My last resistance to the idea of God's wrath was a casualty of the war in former Yugoslavia, the region from which I come. According to estimates, 200,000 people were killed and over 3,000,000 were displaced. My villages and cities were destroyed, my people shelled day in and day out, some of them brutalized beyond imagination, and I could not imagine God not being angry. Or think of Rwanda in the last decade of the past century where 800,000 people were hacked to death in one hundred days! Did God react to the carnage? By refusing to condemn the bloodbath but instead affirming the perpetrator's basic goodness? Wasn't God fiercely angry with them? Though I used to complain about the indecency of the idea of God's wrath, I came to think I would have to rebel against a God who wasn't wrathful at the sight of the world's evil. God isn't wrathful in spite of being love. God is wrathful because God is love.[47]

We may legitimately apply Volf's argument to God's reaction to the atrocities carried out by the Canaanites and ask: Should he not be angry and act accordingly?

Is there love in that 'Old Time Religion'?

Today in many Christian circles it is widely held that God's wrath is more transparent in the Old Testament than his love.[48] But this is far from the case.

In the first place there is much in the Old Testament which speaks of God's love in lofty, moving ways—evidence the book of Hosea, let alone the word most frequently used to describe God's special covenant love is *hesed*. As Dale Ralph Davis has said, 'this is love with 'Velcro' on it'! It is faithful love, sticking by the beloved through thick and thin.

In the second place, the New Testament portrays God's wrath in terms which go much further in their intensity than anything we find in the Old Testament, for example Revelation 6, which draws upon Old Testament war imagery but magnifies and universalises it. What is more, it is Jesus who speaks of God's ultimate judgement in terms of '*gehenna*'—hell—where 'the worm does not die and the fire is not quenched' (Mark 9:48).

The reason why God's wrath appears so stark in the Old Testament is because it is expressed primarily in temporal categories, such as famine, plague, siege, war, slaughter and the like. Not surprisingly, Carson writes, 'in our present focus on here and now, these images have a greater impact upon us than what the New Testament says, with its focus on the afterlife.' He goes on, 'The apostolic writings, climaxing in Revelation 14, offer little support for the view that a kinder, gentler God surfaces in the New Testament at this stage in redemptive history.'[49]

What is needed is a more carefully nuanced understanding of the relationship between God's wrath and love as displayed in the two covenants:

> The reality is that the Old Testament displays the grace and love of God in experience and in types, and these realities become all the clearer in the new covenant writings. Similarly, the Old Testament displays the righteous wrath of God in experience and types, and these realities become all the clearer in the new covenant writings. In other words, both God's love and

God's wrath are ratcheted up in the move from
the old covenant to the new, from the Old
Testament to the New. These themes barrel
along through redemptive history, unresolved
until they come to a resounding climax—in the
cross.[50]

The relevance of the Cross for understanding the Canaanite
'genocide' will be considered in the last chapter, suffice to say
at this stage that the love and wrath of God are not to be
pitted against each other. Strange though it may seem to us,
God's wrath can be understood as an expression of his love
as we have already seen when thinking about a 'jealous'
husband rightly understood. Commenting on the apostle
Paul's statement in Romans 1:18, that 'The wrath of God is
revealed from heaven upon all the godless wickedness of
men', J. A. T. Robinson comments, 'This need not, as
Cranfield stresses, mean attributing to God capricious or
irrational rage, but deeply personal abhorrence, such *love*
[italics mine] must always feel in the presence of injustice or
cruelty.'[51]

Speaking of the Cross raises an important theological
point which we briefly need to consider before moving on.

Much talk of 'the problem of evil' and God's apparent
'injustice' can take place at a rather abstract level. Indeed,
much medieval theology occurred in this way. This was
something Martin Luther railed against in his 'theology of
the Cross'. He argued that if we really want to know what
God is like, we don't begin with speculation but with
revelation, turning to the place where God has made himself
fully and finally known in the person of the Lord Jesus Christ
and in particular at Calvary.

Insight from Jesus

When we consider the specific life of Jesus we are brought 'down to earth' as we are faced with an actual person operating in concrete situations. If Jesus is (as the Bible portrays him to be) God made flesh, then if we want to gain some insight into how God displays his anger and how this co-ordinates with his love, we need to look at the way such anger is displayed by Jesus.

One clear account given in the Gospels of Jesus displaying anger is the cleansing of the temple (e.g. Matthew 21:12-17). Referring to this episode, the nineteenth-century theologian, B. B. Warfield writes:

> Perhaps in no incidents recorded in the Gospels is the action of our Lord's indignation more vividly displayed than in the accounts of the cleansing of the Temple. In closing the account, which he gives earlier of these, John tells us that 'his disciples remembered what was written, "The zeal of thine house shall eat me up"' (John 2:17). The word here employed—'zeal'—may mean nothing more than 'ardour'; but this ardour may burn with hot indignation,—we read of a 'zeal of fire which shall devour the adversaries' (Hebrews 10:27). And it seems to be this hot indignation at the pollution of the house of God—this 'burning jealousy for the holiness of the house of God'—which it connotes in our present passage ... The form in which it here breaks forth is that of indignant anger towards those who defile God's house with trafficking and it thus presents us with one of the most striking manifestations of the anger of Jesus.[52]

What we see concerning God's anger in Jesus of Nazareth is that it is personal and active and so going totally against the likes of Dodd who would portray it as impersonal and passive.

The second inference which can legitimately be drawn is that if God's anger is roused by trafficking goods in the Temple, how much more will it be roused by appalling acts of human abuse which the Bible lays at the door of the Canaanites?

From our discussion so far we can rightly conclude that divine love is compatible with divine anger. What divine love can never be is indifferent.

5. Righteous commands?

Another question which remains to be answered is: Can the commands to be rid of the Canaanites from the land be understood as expressions of God's holy anger, his covenant love and as contributing to his greater purposes for the salvation of the world? Is it possible to see these commands as expressing God's goodness in terms of his righteousness, rather than undermining it?

The Bible passages themselves suggest that they can.

Righteous cleansing not ethnic cleansing

First, the actions against the Canaanites are to be understood within the framework of judicial *punitive* action. God's concern was not simply to have his people located in the land which therefore required the forceful eviction of its present inhabitants, but that the inhabitants were themselves deserving of judgement. As Derek Kidner observes, 'Their justification was not simply that Canaan was earmarked for Israel but that its inhabitants were ripe for judgement.'[53] This is expressed in a variety of ways. In Deuteronomy 9:5 it is put by way of a disclaimer, it is 'not because of your righteousness ... but because of the wickedness of these nations'. Similarly, Deuteronomy 18:12, 'because of these detestable practices the LORD your God will drive out those nations before you.'[54]

Secondly, the action is to be understood as *purgative*. Deuteronomy 20:18 likens the situation to a moral infection which needed to be eradicated 'that they may not teach you their abominable practices'. It would appear that it had reached saturation point, 'Every abominable thing which the LORD hates they have done for their gods; for they even burn their sons and their daughters in the fire of their gods' (Deuteronomy 12:31). Similarly, 'When you enter the land which the LORD your God gives you, you shall not learn to imitate the detestable things of those nations ... because of these detestable things the LORD your God will drive them out before you' (Deuteronomy 18:9,12). As John Stott rightly comments, 'It was essential to protect God's people, who were the recipients of his special revelation, though still at a stage of immaturity (Galatians 4:1-11), from being corrupted by heathen idolatry and immorality.'[55]

Just in case we think this is literally 'overkill' on the part of God (and so a further sign that, in the words of Dawkins, God is 'a vindictive, bloodthirsty ethnic cleanser'), it might be worth pausing to consider the nature of the 'detestable things' which led to such acts of judgement and then consider whether genocide is the proper category within which to understand God's response.

Can it get any worse than this?

Clay Jones has provided clear and extensive evidence of the sort of practices which were occurring in the ancient Near East at the time of the conquest. They make disturbing reading and are not for the fainthearted.[56]

Jones shows that the root of the 'abominable practices' is idolatry; and that far from this being some 'petty, individualistic, private affair', the pervading idolatrous mentality 'was theologically conducive to (if not motivational for) the formation of Canaanite practices, including the practices of incest, adultery, child sacrifice, homosexuality and bestiality, such that these practices are not incoherent with Canaanite idolatry.[57] Elsewhere Jones writes:

> Idolatry perverts our ability to love what Yahweh loves. Consequently, we love what He hates, and we hate what He loves. The story of Canaanite incest, adultery, child sacrifice, homosexuality, and bestiality flow out of the plot line of idolatry. The tragedy of this story is that not only is idolatry an offense to Yahweh, but it fails to supply a happy ending for human communities as well.[58]

Jones points out that as well as divination, witchcraft, and female and male temple sex; Canaanite idolatry involved a wide range of morally repulsive practices which mimicked the sexually perverse conduct of their Canaanite fertility gods: adultery, homosexuality, transvestitism, pederasty (men sexually abusing boys), sex with animals,[59] and incest.

One of the worst practices was that of child sacrifice.

Molech was the Canaanite underworld deity represented as an upright, bull-headed idol with a human body in whose belly a fire was stoked and in whose outstretched arms a child was placed that would be burned to death ... And it was not just infants; children as old as four were sacrificed.[60]

A bronze image of Kronos was set up among them, stretching out its cupped hands above a bronze cauldron, which would burn the child. As the flame burning the child surrounded the body, the limbs would shrivel up and the mouth would appear to grin as if laughing, until it was shrunk enough to slip into the cauldron.[61]

Archaeological evidence indicates that the children burned to death in this way sometimes numbered in the thousands.[62]

What Jones relates as acts by the Canaanites were not occasional peccadilloes carried out by a select few, rather, these practices characterised a whole society from top to bottom. It is therefore difficult to envisage that anything less than a root and branch removal would have been sufficient to deal with such evils.

Can we imagine any Western nation today idly standing by while the mass murder of children in this way was going on in some other part of the world? There would be uproar and a demand for immediate action, and quite rightly so. Why then should we complain that God, the moral ruler of the universe, didn't stand idly by when such practices were going on in Canaan during the time of Joshua but acted in judgement using his people as his judicial instrument?

Jones poses some interesting questions which need to be faced by those who would claim moral outrage at the divine command to rid the land of the Canaanites:

> ... do we genuinely comprehend the depth of Canaanite sins? Do we understand the significance of God's having all but destroyed Israel for committing Canaanite sins? Could it be that because our culture today commits these same Canaanite sins we are inoculated against the seriousness of these sins and so think God's judgement is unfair? How might a theology of

the human heart and its sinful condition illuminate a motivation for 'divine genocide' claims? In short, most of our problems regarding God's ordering the destruction of the Canaanites come from the fact that God hates sin and we do not.[63]

Clearing the way

There is also a third reason for such action by God through his people, namely, that it was *preparatory*, preparing the way for a nation from which a Saviour for the whole world would come.

Yahweh's war was necessary because of the hardness of the heart of the enemy, for the protection of Israel, for the eradication of idolatry, and for the education of Israel and other nations. More than this, it was for the preparation of the nation of Israel to bring forth the One who would come as a Saviour not only for Israel but for all the children of Adam.[64]

It is inconceivable that such conditions could have been achieved without the eradication of Canaanite practices as Israel's history was sadly to show (with its only partial eradication of the Canaanites).[65]

But how are we to understand Israel's part in this? Is it simply an ancient example of 'ethnic cleansing' carried out under the aegis of religious fervour? To help us understand how Israel saw her role we need to explore a little of the special nature of this kind of warfare.

This leads us to consider the notion of the '*herem*' which is translated as 'total destruction' in Deuteronomy 20:17; 'However, in the cities of the nations the LORD your God is giving you as an inheritance, do not leave alive anything that breathes. Completely destroy them—the Hittites, Amorites, Canaanites, Perizzites, Hivites and Jebusites—as the LORD your God has commanded you' (Deuteronomy 20:16-17).

6. A holy war?

Tremper Longman cautions:

> The term *herem* is notoriously difficult to translate. It may be translated 'banned' or 'devoted things'. It refers to plundered items and people captured during the course of holy war. *Herem* involves consecration, the giving over of the captives of war to God. Consecration is a word which suggests worship, and once we understand *herem* warfare in its whole context, we can see just how appropriate that understanding is.[66]

However, J. P. U. Lilley argues that the term 'holy war' is not a biblical one (compared, for example, to 'wars of the Lord'—Numbers 21:14 or 'Yahweh's war') and is therefore misleading. The evidence is that: 'It seems that Israel, like other contemporary societies, did not recognise any distinction between sacred and secular war; as Craigie has said, the label "holy war" is best avoided'.[67] This would mean that any resemblances to Islamic jihad are more apparent than real and so such comparisons are best avoided.

The application of *herem* to the Canaanites is first made in Deuteronomy 7:

> When the LORD your God brings you into the land you are entering to possess and drives out before you many nations—the Hittites, Girgashites, Amorites, Canaanites, Perizzites, Hivites and Jebusites, seven nations larger and stronger than you—and when the LORD your God has delivered them over to you and you have defeated them, then you must destroy them totally. Make no treaty with them, and show them no mercy. Do not intermarry with them. Do not give your daughters to their sons or take their daughters for your sons, for they will turn your children away from following me to serve other gods, and the LORD's anger will burn against you and will quickly destroy you. This is what you are to do to them: Break down their altars, smash their sacred stones, cut down their Asherah poles and burn their idols in the fire... Therefore, take care to follow the commands, decrees and laws I give you today. You must destroy all the peoples the LORD your God gives over to you. Do not look on them with pity and do not serve their gods, for that will be a snare to you Deuteronomy 7:1-5;16.

Then verse 26, 'Do not bring a detestable thing into your house or you, like it, will be set apart for destruction. Regard it as vile and utterly detest it, for it is set apart for destruction.'

The prescriptive phrases (vv1-5, 11, 16, 26), and the promises in v20, echo precisely the terms of Exodus 23:20-33.[68] The verbs 'devote' (v.2) and 'destroy' (v.16) do not appear in Exodus, but 'they shall not live in your land' (Exodus 23:33) has the same practical effect: 'The implications of "devoting" are spelt out: no covenant, no mercy, no intermarriage.'[69]

'In conclusion', writes Lilley:

Where the word *herem/haharim* is used with its full religious force ... it means uncompromising consecration without the possibility of recall or redemption. It was not applied to idolatrous objects, but to things which could have been taken as plunder or people who could have been enslaved. It was not the normal procedure of war, although the verb could be used in a secondary sense to denote overwhelming destruction of the enemy. The application of *herem* did not make a war 'holy'; but it did introduce a special theological dimension which forbade taking booty, or prisoners, or both, according to the instructions given in the particular case.[70]

War as worship

This introduces us to what may seem a rather surprising idea, namely, that such a war is to be understood as part of Israel's *worship* to Yahweh:

The heart of *herem* warfare is the presence of God with his army. Of course, where God is present, he must be worshipped, and thus we will not be surprised to see that *herem* is shaped largely by that fact. Indeed, it is not too strong to say that *herem* warfare is worship. The battlefield is sacred space. To be involved in warfare is a holy activity analogous to the temple.[71]

More recently, G. K. Beale has taken this idea of the command being linked to worship in a slightly different direction in terms of understanding the land as 'sanctuary'.[72] Having described how Eden was conceived as a sanctuary with Adam being commissioned as a king-priest to keep out uncleanness and then to expand this garden sanctuary to the outer regions of the earth, Beale writes:

> Israel was then given the commission to be 'a kingdom of priests' (Exodus 19:6) and to enter the Promised Land and make it into another garden temple by completely cleansing it from the uncleanness of the Canaanites ... Israelite warriors were to wipe out the Canaanites and purify the land, since it was to be pure like the sanctuary of Eden and Israel's temple ... Against this background, God's command to Israel to exterminate Canaanite uncleanness was a commission to wipe out every aspect of impurity ... This is why every idolater, whether young or old or male or female, ideally had to be killed or driven out from the land.

Beale then adds a very important proviso, 'this was a unique and unrepeatable commission, which in no way applies after the epoch of Israel's theocracy.'[73] In other words, the command to Israel to act in this way was highly specific and limited, it is what can be labelled *sui generis* (a class all of its own) and so cannot be taken as a model for either the church or other 'religious' nations to act in the same way. Christopher Wright is surely correct when he says that the conquest of Canaan 'was never meant to become a model for how all future generation were to behave towards their contemporary enemies.'[74]

That Israel was to conduct any future wars differently to the conquest of Canaan is made explicit in Deuteronomy 20:10:

> When you march up to attack a city, make its people an offer of peace. If they accept and open their gates, all the people in it shall be subject to forced labour and shall work for you. If they refuse to make peace and they engage you in battle, lay siege to that city. When the LORD your God delivers it into your hand, put to the sword all the men in it. As for the women, the children, the livestock and everything else in the city, you may take these as plunder for yourselves.

Similarly, Kevin J. Vanhoozer notes, 'The *herem*—the requirement to "dedicate" the Canaanites to destruction—ultimately pertains to holiness, not hostility: "It was not driven by genocidal or military considerations, but the need to eradicate evil and prevent evil from spreading to the new population."'[75]

The biblical perspective has priority

This understanding establishes several important points which help us view the Canaanite conquest from the biblical perspective rather than our own Western twenty-first-century one.

First, this is not nationalistic expansionism of the kind Hitler engaged in, and so Dawkins' parallel collapses at this point.

Second, the timing is significant. Israel was made to wait four hundred years until it would be right to invade, for until then 'the iniquity of the Amorites was not yet full' (Genesis 15:16). As Kidner observes:

> It implies that to have seized the inheritance prematurely would have been no better than robbery—promise or no promise. So at the beginning of their history the people of God were taught that divine patronage confers no moral exemptions. Not all modern nations have shown such scruples ... This is not nationalism.[76]

This display of God's patience in waiting four hundred years also puts paid to the claim that God is a 'capriciously malevolent bully'. What kind of bully is this patient?!

Third, the fundamental framework within which to understand these commands is that of covenant obedience and worship. Therefore, in addition to his judicial wrath we should expect to see some of those other divine characteristics such as longsuffering and mercy mentioned in Exodus 34.

This is, in fact, what we do find. We have already drawn attention to God's holiness as well as his patience and mercy being 'goods'. In this particular instance, the 'good' which God desires is that the land which is to be occupied is removed of repulsive and destructive practices. In their place there is to be righteousness with a view to Israel being a light to all the nations (a theme especially taken up later by Isaiah and its future eschatological fulfilment—Isaiah 60:1-3; 62:1-3). In short, the good is purity. As Beale argues, the land is to be a new sanctuary, a kind of new Eden.

But there is also the element of mercy. Interestingly enough, in less extreme kinds of warfare the kings of Israel had a name among their enemies for mercy (1 Kings 20:31). Restraints in warfare were both implicit and explicit, so for enemies who were not appointed for utter destruction (*herem*) there must be no 'scorched earth' policy employed, (Deuteronomy 20:19f). Furthermore, before a city was besieged it was to be offered peace conditions which compare favourably with the brutal terms of, for instance, the Ammonites in 1 Samuel 11:2. However, as Kidner points out, we have to be careful not to exaggerate this moderation, for:

> If a city opted to fight, and was taken, all its males except the children were to be put to the sword' (Deuteronomy 20:13). Even this, however, may conceal an understanding that it applied to those who still would not surrender, since we find that in practice the Israelites took prisoners in normal warfare, and considered it unthinkable to kill them (2 Kings 6:22).[77]

There is also the striking example of the sparing of Rahab and her family who were then welcomed into the ranks of Israel (Joshua 2). This is not only illustrative of God's mercy but acts as a counter to those who would claim that in the Canaanite conquest we have an instance of ethnic cleansing. P. J. Williams suggests that it would be fair to deduce from this incident that had all the other Canaanites turned to Yahweh, they too would have been rescued.[78]

Koukl goes so far as to claim that this brings into question the suitability of applying the term 'genocide' at all with its racist or nationalistic associations.[79]

Compare and contrast

It is also worth pointing out that what is considered to be merciful is to some degree relative. Here we must bear in mind the cultural norms of the day when engaging in warfare and not compare them to twenty-first-century practices with things like the Geneva Convention operating. When we set these alongside the practices of Israel we do see Israel showing restraint to a remarkable degree. A quick putting to the sword stands in stark contrast to this description of the practice of the later Assyrian King Ashurbanipal II:

> Ashurbanipal's usual procedure after the capture of a hostile city was to burn it and then to mutilate all the male prisoners by cutting off their hands and ears and putting out their eyes after which they were put in a great heap to perish from torture from sun, flies, their wounds and suffocation. The children, boys and girls were all burnt alive at the stake and the chief was carried off to Assyria to be flayed alive for the king's delectation.[80]

Perhaps the reputation of Israel in 1 Kings 20:31 was justified after all! 'His officials said to him, "Look, we have heard that the kings of Israel are merciful. Let us go to the king of Israel with sackcloth around our waists and ropes around our heads. Perhaps he will spare your life."' This provides us with some measure of cultural perspective by which to evaluate Israel's actions as decreed by God.

It might also be proposed that it was the expulsion of the Canaanites from the land which was the intended punishment by God, not their annihilation, in which case the term 'genocide' is hardly appropriate.

Coulter argues that:

> There is a range of verbs used in the commands to Israel concerning how they should treat the Canaanites. Some of these clearly speak of extermination, but others speak of driving them

out (see Deuteronomy 7). Deuteronomy 9:3 brings these two ideas together succinctly: 'You will drive them out and annihilate them quickly, as the LORD has promised you'. It seems, from a careful reading of the related passages that God's intention was that the Canaanites would have a possibility of fleeing the land as the Israelites advanced. In the case of those kings and cities that refused to do so, there was no option but annihilation. There is no suggestion that Canaanites who left the land must be pursued; rather, the commands to annihilate are connected only with people in the cities of the land. Presumably, if the Canaanites had left Canaan they would then have been treated like all other nations and the Israelites could have made treaties with them and would have been bound by the more general codes of conduct in warfare given in Deuteronomy 20.[81]

Coulter expounds this point further:

So, this was not so much a case of *genocide* (the extermination of an ethnic group) but rather *forced removal from the land of Canaan* [italics mine]. God's judgement was primarily that the Canaanites would lose the land because of their detestable religious practices and in order to preserve the purity of Israel's worship of Him. As we read through Joshua and Judges this appears to be borne out, as the extermination of the Canaanites is never fully implemented ... This understanding that the primary nature of the judgement was expulsion from the land helps us to understand Leviticus 18:24-29 where God says, 'the land vomited out its inhabitants' and that if the Israelites copy the religions of

Canaan, the land, 'will vomit you out as it vomited out the nations that were before you'. The judgement against Israel, when it came, was not annihilation but exile from the land. Joshua 12 lists 31 kings who were defeated by Joshua and whose cities were therefore wiped out (at this time the Canaanites lived largely in independent walled city-states).[82]

Even if all of this were to be granted, understandably there is moral recoil against the idea that children were to be included in this.

7. What about the children?

Some scholars like William Lane Craig raise the possibility that Canaanite children were not actually killed since there is no record of this in the biblical text.[83] Paul Copan points out that while there is the command to kill whoever is there, that doesn't necessarily mean that Israel killed women and children.[84] Similarly John Goldingay writes: 'When a city is in danger of falling, people do not simply wait there to be killed; they get out ... Only people who do not get out, such as the city's defenders, get killed.'[85] However, Craig does acknowledge the possibility (if not the probability), that children were involved in such action. This does seem highly likely.

Sin which weaves a web

As we approach this subject in a spirit of humility, it is important to appreciate the corporate and collective nature of sin and that which it brings in its wake—judgement. The reality is that the consequences of sin are not always discriminating. The wanton pillaging of the environment by one generation can often have dire effects on the next who themselves had not been involved in their making. Leaders of a nation may go to war for just or unjust reasons, but in so doing they bring with them into the conflict the rest of the nation.

In modern times the Spanish Civil War was the first 'total war' with civilians finding themselves on the front line, including children. As D. A. Carson observes:

> The consequences of human sin infest many of our experiences with some measure of pain. Such afflictions may be splashed onto the canvas of human history with a very broad brush. Thus God says to Jerusalem, 'I am against you. I will draw my sword from its scabbard and cut off from you both the righteous and the wicked' (Ezekiel 21:3). In one sense, of course, no one is righteous (Romans 3:10ff); but that is not what the prophet means here. He means that when devastation descends on Jerusalem, the people who will suffer will include those whose immediate sins have brought the city to this horrible punishment, and those who have not participated in the sins that have brought about the destruction of the nation ... War, plague, congenital birth defects and many other afflictions are like that: they are not very discriminating. Therefore if we see them only as retaliation or retribution for specific sins, we shall be terribly confused when people who have not indulged in such sins suffer along with those who have. But if instead we see such suffering as, in the first place, the effluent of the fall, the result of a fallen world, the consequences of evil that is really evil and in which we ourselves all too frequently indulge, then however much we

may grieve when we suffer, we will not be taken
by surprise.[86]

We might note too how in the prophecy of Ezekiel it is the
LORD who depicts himself as a warrior who will inflict such
destruction upon the whole nation, including children, using
another nation, in this case Babylon, as his judicial
instrument. The parallel, therefore, with the Canaanite
conquest is all the more striking.

When you look at film footage of the utter devastation
wreaked upon the German cities of Berlin and Dresden
during the Second World War, (and without for a moment
engaging in any sense of moral superiority) it is difficult not
to entertain the thought that whilst it was allied bombers
that were the immediate cause of such carnage, at a deeper
level it was the Nazi leadership and those adults who had
supported them who were ultimately to blame. If so, then it
could legitimately be said that they brought the destruction
down upon their own heads (and that of their children).

Although such words may grate with our modern
sensibilities as we hear them from a distance in time of over
70 years, the chilling speech of Air Marshall Sir Arthur
('Bomber') Harris, conveys the stark reality of the
'boomerang' effects of rampant evil:

> The Nazis entered this war under the rather
> childish delusion that they were going to bomb
> everyone else, and nobody was going to bomb
> them. At Rotterdam, London, Warsaw, and half
> a dozen other places, they put their rather naive
> theory into operation. They sowed the wind,
> and now they are going to reap the whirlwind.

Similarly, given the evidence provided by Clay Jones
concerning the sickening evils being perpetrated by

Canaanite society, anyone who takes the biblical portrayal of God's holiness at all seriously, should not be at all surprised that 'the wages of sin' which is 'death', was experienced by the whole nation.

A severe mercy?

Paul Coulter suggests that the means of judgement (which he takes to be physical annihilation and not simply the ejection from the land) could be considered merciful: 'Although the killing of children by the sword seems brutal to us, it was relatively merciful compared with the alternatives of abandonment and starvation. The sword is actually a quick and relatively painless means of execution.'[87] Here the principle of cultural/moral relativity comes into play as mentioned earlier when comparing that which was required by the Israelites and the standard method of torture and butchery carried out by the likes of Assyrian King Ashurbanipal II.

Another consideration is the weighting of potential greater evils and hidden greater goods. For many in the West, death is seen as that which is to be avoided at all costs such that it is difficult to envisage anything worse than death. This is especially so when it comes to our children. As a father, I would not even give it a moment's thought if I were to be asked to sacrifice my life for that of my children or grandchildren. But what if I were to be able to look into the future and that future was one in which my children were to grow up to do terrible evils? Then an early death, (if that is the only option) may not seem so terrible after all. Here a lesser evil (premature death) is to be preferred over a greater evil (a life of wickedness).

If this is linked to the belief put forward by the likes of William Lane Craig and Greg Koukl that babies and infants go to be with God after death, then the perspective is changed yet again.

Lane argues that the death of the Canaanite children was also their salvation, saved from a life of appalling corruption and saved to be with God. This possibility is also proposed by Coulter but with an added cautionary note:

> If we ask whether it would be better for God to allow children to grow up in such a perverted culture and religious system or to bring their young lives to an end and gather them to Himself, we begin to see that what happened to them may not have been the worst option. Even as we consider this, however, we are on dangerous ground. Only God can make this kind of judgement, since He alone possesses all knowledge and wisdom. Our finite minds are incapable of understanding every dimension of such a dilemma. Like Paul, we must acknowledge that God's judgements are unsearchable and His paths are 'beyond tracing out' (Romans 11:33). A humble submission to God's wisdom at this point seems the most appropriate response given the paucity of the biblical data on the issue.[88]

One final comment needs to be made which is relevant to our discussion.

We have seen that from a Scriptural standpoint sin has a corporate effect with some degree of collective guilt being accrued. In his 'strange work' of wrath, God also shows mercy, as we have seen, even to a culture as morally degenerate as that of the Canaanites. As such it is questionable whether the Bible does see children as 'innocents' in an absolute sense, something taken up by Tremper Longman;

> We must point out that the Bible does not understand the destruction of men, women and children of these cities as a slaughter of innocents. Not even the children are considered innocent. They are all part of an inherently wicked culture that, if allowed to live, would morally and theologically pollute the people of Israel. The passage in Joshua 6 (21) ... was prefaced by the motivation to avoid their own destruction. Indeed, from the perspective of the Bible, God had practiced great patience with the people who lived in Palestine. The reason why the descendants of Abraham had to wait so long before entering the Promised Land was because 'the sin of the Amorites has not yet reached its full measure.'[89]

As we shall see, the issue of children suffering due to the 'sins of their fathers' is not alleviated in the New Testament, if anything, it is accentuated.

8. The wider New Testament perspective

Earlier the claim was made by D. A. Carson that far from God's wrath being restricted to the Old Testament only to be replaced by his love in the New, both undergo a 'ratcheting up' until they come together at the Cross of Christ. Carson's observation that one of the reasons why we find the expression of God's wrath so difficult to come to terms with in the Old Testament is because of its temporal manifestations (in our space and time) is an important one. But it is also vital to recognise that even in the New Testament material/temporal expressions of God's judgement are to be found.

We shall briefly explore two of these, one from Luke's Gospel and the other from the book of Revelation in order to show that the Canaanite episode can't be written off as either never having occurred or being the result of a misunderstanding of God on the part of the Israelites.

Luke 12:49-13:9—troops and towers

This poignant episode in the life of Jesus is set against the backdrop of his warning of God's impending judgement:

He said to the crowd: 'When you see a cloud rising in the west, immediately you say, "It's going to rain," and it does. And when the south wind blows, you say, "It's going to be hot," and it is. Hypocrites! You know how to interpret the appearance of the earth and the sky. How is it that you don't know how to interpret this present time?' Luke 12:54-56

Jesus has been teaching from the beginning of chapter 12 that judgement for the nation of Israel is just around the corner and that since he has come into the world, people are left without excuse. God's King has arrived and he now calls people to acknowledge the Son of Man (v.8). The moment that happens, he says, judgement and division occur, v.49: 'I have come to bring fire on the earth', then v.51: 'Do you think that I have come to bring peace on earth? No, I tell you, but division.' He then goes on to speak about the way families will be divided along lines of allegiance to him; those who are for him and those who are against him with the result that the whole human race is split down the middle. These are constitutive of the signs of the times to Israel. 'Look', says Jesus in effect, 'You pride yourself on being weather watchers. You can tell when a storm is brewing or when the drought is on its way and you prepare accordingly. Then why are you being so wilfully blind now? Can't you see that God is doing something extraordinary and new? All the signs are there staring you in the face if only you would have eyes to see. If someone is taking you to court, you know that the best thing to do is to settle matters before you get there, because if not you run the risk of paying the full penalty. Similarly, judgement day is coming and now is the time to get things sorted out with God who is the ultimate judge.' This is in part the point of the little story in vv.57-59:

> Why don't you judge for yourselves what is
> right? As you are going with your adversary to
> the magistrate, try hard to be reconciled to him
> on the way, or he may drag you off to the judge,
> and the judge turn you over to the officer, and
> the officer throw you into prison. I tell you, you
> will not get out until you have paid the last
> penny.

Tragically, the leaders of Israel did not listen. The Messiah
was rejected and Jerusalem was judged when in AD 70 it was
razed to the ground with merciless brutality by the Romans.
In this they were to see the hand of God (13:35). These events
of judgement are in some measure comparable to the
judgement God inflicted upon the Canaanites.[90]

Jesus then goes on to relate God's future judgement to
present events in which people are meant to see God's hand
at work:

> Now there were some present at that time who
> told Jesus about the Galileans whose blood
> Pilate had mixed with their sacrifices. Jesus
> answered, 'Do you think that these Galileans
> were worse sinners than all the other Galileans
> because they suffered this way? I tell you, no!
> But unless you repent, you too will all perish. Or
> those eighteen who died when the tower in
> Siloam fell on them—do you think they were
> more guilty than all the others living in
> Jerusalem? I tell you, no! But unless you repent,
> you too will all perish. (13:1-5)

Here were two tragic occurrences which were on the minds
of Jesus' audience which repulsed them, as the narratives of
the Canaanite expulsions repulse many today.

The first is man-made; a massacre. The Roman governor Pilate, known for taking a hard line on political disturbances, had allowed his troops to go on the rampage killing Galilean Jews when they were about to perform a sacred religious duty, probably the Passover sacrifice. These were not particularly immoral people; they were religious people to whom this happened. Why, then, did God allow it? What is more, given that these were Galilean Jews, it is highly likely that some of them would have been known to Jesus personally, he would have grown up with some as a boy and he would have travelled with them to the religious festivals (Luke 2:41-44). This issue for Jesus and his audience was not theoretical and abstract but personal and practical.

The second event is more of a 'natural disaster', the collapse of a tower killing eighteen people. This too may have had a religious connection because the tower was next to the pool of Siloam just several hundred metres south of the Temple area in Jerusalem. According to the Talmud, water was drawn up from Siloam's pool in a golden vessel to be carried in procession to the temple on the Jewish Feast of the Tabernacles. We may speculate that it was during this procession, which would have taken them past the tower that this happened. If this is the case, then more 'good' religious folk were killed.

Often with a sense of self-righteousness we look at human suffering and demand of God: 'What are you going to do about it?' 'How can God be good?' But Jesus looks at tragedy in quite a different light and asks significantly different questions. He plays it back to his enquirers and asks: 'What are you going to do about it? In the light of the precarious nature of life, how can you be so bad, complacently living as if life is meant to be happy and carefree with no personal accountability to your Maker?'

The Christian speaker Ravi Zacharias gives an illuminating illustration of this same approach. He relates how he was on a radio talk show at Ohio University when a woman stood up to shout him down. She yelled, 'I know what this is all about. You are trying to take away my moral right to make my decisions over whether I can abort what is in my womb.' In fact, he hadn't even mentioned the topic of abortion; he had been talking about the origin of the universe! The woman pressed her attack, 'I know what you Christians are trying to do—take away my right as a woman to do with my body as I please.' Ravi Zacharias replied, 'Since you have brought it up, I find it interesting that you have worded it this way. You call this "your moral right". You know, if a plane was to suddenly crash and 90 people died and 10 people lived then you would be asking, "What kind of God is this who chooses who should live and who should die? I can't believe in this kind of God, he must be evil"' He then went on to say, 'I find this fascinating, when God makes a selective judgement on the basis of his sovereign knowledge you call him evil. At the same time when you make a judgement to do away with life in your womb you call it your moral right. Can you explain this conundrum to me?'

We are to notice that Jesus doesn't assume that those who died did not in some way deserve their fate. The fact that he turns to the crowd and urges them to repent or they too might perish indicates that in Jesus' mind at least death is in some way or another linked to sin. Rebellion against God is the human scandal and death is the divine verdict.

However, it would be a mistake to draw the wrong conclusion that particular sufferings are a result of particular sins (this was the faulty thinking which characterised Job's 'comforters').[91] In this passage Jesus insists that there is no evidence that those who suffer in this way were more wicked than anyone else but simply that if the same were to happen to others it would be no more than they deserve: 'Do you think that these Galileans were worse sinners than all the other Galileans because they suffered this way?' (v.2). And again in v.4, 'Or those eighteen who died when the tower in Siloam fell on them—do you think they were more guilty than all the others living in Jerusalem?' The answer Jesus gives to both questions is a resounding 'No!' But that doesn't mean that others deserve anything less—v.3: 'But unless you repent, you too will all perish.' This means there is no room for smug moral superiority by anyone, looking down upon those who are suffering as if they especially deserve it and we do not. We are all on the wrong side of our Maker, our relationship with him is dead and physical death is a poignant reminder of that lamentable fact.

Of course, we do not know the tone in which Jesus spoke when challenging the crowd: 'Repent or you too will perish.' But since we are told in the book of Isaiah that he was to be a man who would 'not break a bruised reed or snuff a smouldering wick' (42:3 cf. Matthew 12:17-21) we can be quietly confident that it was with compassion in his voice and tears in his eyes as we see later in v.34 as he agonises over Jerusalem's refusal to repent. Would it be too much of a leap of the imagination to say that such was God's reaction to the necessary removal of the Canaanites?

In this episode we see another point of contact with the conquest narratives, namely, the presence of mercy. God waited 400 years before judgement was carried out. Rahab and others were spared, so it is here that an extended period of grace is being offered: 'A man had a fig tree, planted in his vineyard, and he went to look for fruit on it, but did not find any. So he said to the man who took care of the vineyard, "For three years now I've been coming to look for fruit on this fig tree and haven't found any. Cut it down! Why should it use up the soil?" "Sir," the man replied, "leave it alone for one more year, and I'll dig around it and fertilize it. If it bears fruit next year, fine! If not, then cut it down."' (vv.6-9).

The meaning of the parable is not difficult to discern. The vineyard is Israel (cf. Isaiah 5), God is the owner and Israel's God-intended purpose was to be a witness to the world so that non-Jews would come to know the one true God. Her fruit should have been wholesome and attractive. She was now in danger of forfeiting that position by becoming inward-looking and exclusive, especially in rejecting the Messiah. God through his Son is warning her of the consequences before it is too late.

If God thinks that our eternal value is such that he considers it worth lifting his restraining hand in order to permit tragedies to happen in our world so that we seek the One who alone can fix the deeper tragedy of our alienation from him (as this episode illustrates), and we judge that hard, then we might think on this: in but a few weeks after this incident Jesus is going to go to Jerusalem and before a watching world will undergo the greatest agony of all—the agony of the Cross.

Derek Kidner also draws attention to the view that what happened in Canaan was the shape of things to come:

> So our Lord viewed them—not as 'old, unhappy,
> far-off things', confined to the Old Testament

and to a tribal god long superseded. In the human story, disasters and wars would continue to the end. As it had been in the days of Noah, so would it be in the end; for the Old Testament had shown only a foretaste; the full reality lay ahead. Even when challenged, Jesus refused to moralise or philosophise on the human violence or natural disasters of His day, for he saw them not as problems but as signs of a world ready to perish, and as a summons to repentance (Luke 13:1-15).[92]

In this passage we have the same elements as in the conquest of Canaan: God exercises patience with rebellious people, but when such patience is not met with repentance God's judgement is executed. Mercy is extended, but judgement will eventually fall.

Revelation 6—The wrath of the Lamb

Albeit a different genre (what is called 'apocalyptic'), the book of Revelation deals with the same themes as Jesus in Luke 13 and the conquest of Canaan in the Pentateuch, namely, God's wrathful and merciful response to a wayward world. In particular, chapter 6 sheds light on the role war plays as an instrument of God's righteous anger and severe mercy.

Prior to the Great War, the European intelligentsia believed civilisation was on the verge of a new age of peace and prosperity to be ushered in by modern science. This is amply illustrated by two publications of the time.

First, there is Norman Angell's *The Great Illusion*, published in 1909 which went on to be a bestseller. He argued that the great democracies of Europe were 'losing the psychological impulse for war.' He went on to say that 'The least informed of us realises that the whole trend of history is against the tendency to attack the ideals and beliefs of other men.'[93] There was to be a new age of international cooperation using our resources for peaceful purposes rather than the preparation of war. 'How can we possibly expect to keep alive warlike qualities,' he asked, 'when all our interests and activities—all our environments, in short, are peace-like?'[94]

The second is the 1914 edition of the Peace Yearbook of Britain's National Peace Council which predicted:

> Peace, the babe of the nineteenth century, is the strong youth of the twentieth century; for War, the product of anarchy and fear, is passing away under the growing and persistent pressure of world organisation, economic necessity, human intercourse and that change of spirit, that social sense and newer aspect of worldwide life which is the insistent note, the Zeitgeist of the age.[95]

Despite the veneer of religion, immorality and smugness held sway, not least amongst the ruling classes. When the storm of war eventually broke upon an unsuspecting world, many people were totally bewildered. It was then that the weak moral optimism favoured by theological liberalism was exposed as the superficial sham it was. In 1916, the Congregationalist preacher, P. T. Forsyth wrote:

> World calamity bears home to us the light way in which, through a long peace and insulation, we were coming to take the problem of the world and especially its moral problem. 'We do not bother about sin' we said with some satisfaction. The preachers protested in vain against that terrible statement—those of them

that had not lost their Gospel. But they were damned with the charge of theology. And now God enters the pulpit and preaches in His own way by deeds [he is speaking of the war]. And his sermons are long and taxing and they spoil the dinner. Clearly God's problem with the world is much more serious than we had dreamed. We are having a revelation of the awful and desperate nature of evil ... We see more of the world Christ saw. It calls for a vaster salvation and a diviner Christ than we were sinking to believe.[96]

War and natural catastrophes are meant to shake a nation into repentance (as should have happened with the Canaanites—and in the case of Rahab did happen), and God would rather have us being rudely shaken from our plight than for us to quietly drift off into a spiritual slumber only to wake up in hell—either a hellish society (like that of the Canaanites) or actual hell itself.

In reflecting on the events of 9/11 and the Twin Towers, Anne Graham Lotz captured this same biblical sentiment when she wrote:

I was watching television the first day and interviewed a construction worker who had been an eyewitness through all of this in a building next to the World Trade Centre. He said, 'I've seen planes hit this building, people falling out of the sky'. He said, 'my heart is in my throat'. I feel like I would say the same thing. You almost don't have thoughts to articulate. Your heart is in your throat. You can hardly stand it. You're numb. For myself, I fall back on my faith in God and the foundation, speaking of those buildings, as an illustration of America, our foundation is our faith in God and the structure we build on that foundation is what enables us to endure something like this ... I believe God also knows what it is like to lose a loved one, gave his only son on a cross. He knows what it is like to see a loved one die a horrific death. He's emotionally involved in our pain and he has the answers to us and he can bring comfort beyond human understanding. Well, I pray that God will use this event to change us forever in a positive way. And that will strengthen our faith in him. I thought of all those people who have died in this tragedy. It doesn't matter right now what political affiliation they had or what denomination they belong to or what religion or what the colour of their skin was or their stock portfolio. What matters is their relationship with God. I would like to see Americans begin to focus on some of the primary things and some of the things that are more important than just, you know, entertainment and pleasure and making more money.

The belief that God so passionately loves his world that he will resort to what C. S. Lewis called 'the megaphone of pain' is to the forefront of chapter 6 of the book of Revelation, in particular what is referred to as 'the wrath of the Lamb' (v. 16).

At first sight this seems a strange term. Can we imagine anyone being so scared of a little lamb that they cry out, 'May the mountains and rocks fall on us'? But this is no ordinary lamb; it is a symbol of the crucified, risen and ascended Lord Jesus, whom we have been introduced to in chapter 1 as having eyes which blaze like fire, and feet like bronze glowing in a furnace, from whose mouth comes a sharp, double-edged sword (note the 'warrior' imagery). He is the one, we are told in chapter 5, who is the Lion of Judah, a royal figure, who is also the Lamb that was slain to take away the sins of the world.

In chapters 4 and 5 we have been presented with a vision of God on his throne which underscores that the Triune God is Sovereign ruler. In chapter 6 we begin to see some of the entailments of that rule.

In chapter 5, we find Jesus, the Lion who is the lamb, taking from God's right hand a scroll. What the content of that scroll is we see a little later at the beginning of chapter 10. But in chapter 6, and throughout chapter 8 and the trumpet blasts, we observe what happens as the scroll begins to be progressively opened by the Lord Jesus Christ, as one by one the seven seals are broken to reveal the purposes of God to bring into effect salvation and judgement in his world. The events that follow the breaking of each seal are not the contents of the scroll itself, they act as triggers to heighten the tension leading us on to a climax in chapter 10 when the scroll is finally opened and all is revealed.[97] That is, these events on earth accompany the opening of the scroll.

What, then, are the sort of things which are going to be happening in our world by divine 'say so' and what are they intended to achieve?

In verses 1-8 we have the famous 'four horsemen of the apocalypse':

> I watched as the Lamb opened the first of the seven seals. Then I heard one of the four living creatures say in a voice like thunder, "Come!" I looked, and there before me was a white horse! Its rider held a bow, and he was given a crown,

and he rode out as a conqueror bent on conquest.

When the Lamb opened the second seal, I heard the second living creature say, "Come!" Then another horse came out, a fiery red one. Its rider was given power to take peace from the earth and to make men slay each other. To him was given a large sword.

When the Lamb opened the third seal, I heard the third living creature say, "Come!" I looked, and there before me was a black horse! Its rider was holding a pair of scales in his hand. Then I heard what sounded like a voice among the four living creatures, saying, "A quart of wheat for a day's wages, and three quarts of barley for a day's wages, and do not damage the oil and the wine!"

When the Lamb opened the fourth seal, I heard the voice of the fourth living creature say, "Come!" I looked, and there before me was a pale horse! Its rider was named Death, and Hades was following close behind him. They were given power over a fourth of the earth to kill by sword, famine and plague, and by the wild beasts of the earth.

The first horse is white, symbolising victory which we can deduce from the rest of the verse which refers to the rider wearing a crown and conquering. The second horse to appear is red; this is the colour of war and bloodshed. The third horse is black, the colour of famine and pestilence. The fourth horse is said to be pale. The word used is one from which we get our word, 'chlorine', it is a greenish white, the colour of a corpse—thus representing death. All of these are worked out in the vision. There is the domination of nations by conquest and the slaughter of people by war. There is also the ravage of whole populations through famine, leading to inflated prices (v.6). All of which lead to death—the rider of the corpse-coloured horse—the culmination of all the previous three, 'They were given power over a fourth of the earth to kill by sword, famine and plague, and by the wild beasts of the earth'(v.8).

There are two things in particular to notice about this vision which are relevant to our wider discussion about God's dealings with the Canaanites.

The first is that it is God who decrees these things to happen. This is shown in two ways. First, it is the four living creatures, the higher orders of angels who in voices like thunder cry, 'Come' and then the horse rides out on the earth. Like all angels they are God's messengers issuing God's commands. Second, the four horsemen appear as a result of Jesus the Lamb opening a seal—he activates the event whether it be war, famine, or death. The truth is clear: God is sovereign over all things and an expression of that is his display of righteous anger in the world.

Secondly, we are to notice that the devastation which follows is not total but limited; it was only a quarter of the earth affected (v8). Again we are not to think of this literally, it serves the purpose of pointing to the reality that whatever judgement God might be carrying out on the earth, it is neither total nor final. What is more, by limiting the judgement God is actually showing the world mercy. This is what we have also seen operating in the Canaanite conquest.

Both these New Testament accounts of the temporal nature of God's judgement have been relayed in some detail in order to offset the often heard objection that the God of the Old Testament is different from the God portrayed in the

New Testament. Clearly, this is not the case. God's self-revelation is consistent and coherent, with it becoming clearer in the New Testament. Both Testaments portray God who, in his holiness, is implacably opposed to all sin which issues in judgement, and yet in his love shows mercy which calls for repentance. That was the case with the Canaanites in the ancient world as it is with Americans and Europeans in the modern world. It is a matter of 'reading the times' correctly through the lens of God's revelation of Scripture.

9. Present wickedness and future judgement

Something else which links the Old Testament case of the Canaanites, God's present revelation of his wrath (Romans 1:18ff) and the future judgement to come, is what Meredith Kline calls 'intrusion ethics'.[98] Kline reminds his readers that rebellion (and all sin is lawlessness according to 1 John 3:4) leads to death (Genesis 2:17). It is only because of God's wonderful grace that Adam and Eve were not killed on the spot when they disobeyed God by eating the fruit of the tree. It is that same grace (common grace) which is extended to us all so that we still live and, by and large thrive in God's world. Within this perspective it is not that we should be astounded that God ordered the death of the Canaanites, but that he allows anyone to live. According to Kline, the conquest of Canaan involves the intrusion of the ethics of the end times into the period of common grace. If this is so then we can see how the destruction of the Canaanites is an anticipation and preview of the final judgement yet to come.

Same yet different

There is both continuity and discontinuity between the
Testaments. It is not, however, a discontinuity of the
revelation of God and his ways, with the crude 'God of wrath'
being replaced by the kindly 'God of love', the error of
Marcion. It is rather that some of the outworkings of God's
revelation, in terms of his holy love which are culturally
specific (judgement against the Canaanites and at the same
time the fulfilment of his covenantal promises to Israel),
become transposed and universalised in the New Testament
through the person and work of Jesus Christ.

Tremper Longman traces the continuity/discontinuity
between the two Testaments in terms of *herem* warfare and
shows how such a transposition might take place and
concludes:

> The God of the Old Testament is not a different
> God from the God we encounter in the New
> Testament. Nor did God change his mind. The
> war against the Canaanites was simply an early
> phase of the battle that comes to its climax on
> the cross and its completion at the final
> judgement. The object of warfare moves from
> the Canaanites, who are the object of God's
> wrath for their sin, to the spiritual powers and
> principalities, and then finally on to the utter
> destruction of all evil, human and spiritual.
> Indeed, it must be said that those who have
> moral difficulties with the genocide in the
> conquest of Canaan should have even more
> serious difficulties with the final judgement. In
> the latter, all those who do not follow Christ will
> be thrown into the lake of fire. The alternatives
> to embracing this picture are either, rejecting

the biblical God or playing the Marcionite game of choosing those Scriptures which suit us, or perhaps treating the final judgement as a metaphor for total annihilation. However, even the latter is not a pleasant thought and still raises issues about how a loving God can exercise any kind of penalty toward the wicked.[99]

We have seen that one of the primary reasons given for the eradication of the Canaanites from the land was that of judicial punishment because of the dreadful wickedness being perpetrated by them. Before we hasten to conclude that God should have shown more leniency (bearing in mind the 400 year wait before judgement was finally executed), it might be worth reflecting on our instinctive cries for justice when we come across cases which are not that dissimilar to the sort of things which were taking place in Canaan but on a far grander scale.

For example, here is part of Elie Wiesel's chilling testimony of what he saw happening in Auschwitz:

> The other gas chambers were full of adults and therefore the children were not gassed, but just burned alive. There were several thousand of them. When one of the SS sort had pity on the children, he would take a child and beat the head against a stone before putting it on the pile of fire and wood, so that the child lost consciousness. However, the regular way they did it was by just throwing the children on the pile. They would put a sheet of wood there, then sprinkle the whole thing with petrol, then wood again, and petrol and wood and petrol—then they placed the children there. Then the whole thing was lighted.[100]

Are we not to think that God did not hear those screams and will not call those evil perpetrators to account? This is not too distant a parallel to what the Canaanites were doing with their children for religious purposes. As the world looked on unbelievingly at the horror of the Holocaust, perhaps if we could see the horror of the Holocaust committed in Canaan we might begin to get a little closer to understanding why the Bible describes the Canaanites who burned their children alive as an 'abomination' (Deuteronomy 12:31).

Cries to heaven for hell

When we are faced with such evils there does appear to be an inner deep-seated sense that in some cases no punishment will ever fit the crime. The Christian sociologist, Peter Berger, notes how in the debate over the architect of Hitler's Jewish extermination programme, Adolf Eichmann, there was a general feeling that 'hanging was not enough'. He points out that in the case of some human deeds no human punishment will ever be enough. He writes: 'It's our experience in which our sense of what is humanly permissible is so fundamentally outraged that the only adequate response to the offence as to the offender seems to be a curse of supernatural dimensions.' He goes on to say that, 'deeds that cry out to heaven also cry out for hell'.[101] In other words, there are deeds which demand not only divine condemnation but divine damnation. It was Winston Churchill who once said that the evidence that 'God existed was the existence of Lenin and Trotsky, for whom hell was needed'.

If this is a deeply rooted instinctive human reaction to evil, which we feel is justified, why should we expect anything less from the fount and measure of all goodness and justice—God? If we often desire justice to be swift and exact (even settling for 'rough justice' if the deeds are deemed sufficiently evil) then can God be considered to be acting prematurely if he waits four centuries until the 'sins of the Amorites have reached their full measure'?

Sometimes the impression is given by the Bible's critics that when it comes to God, a 'heads we win, tails he loses' stance is adopted. If God does not act towards evil in the world, we accuse him of being indifferent or amoral (or cite his apparent inactivity as evidence that he doesn't exist). But when it is claimed that he does act, as in the case of the Canaanites, we think his action too harsh and accuse him of mass murder.[102]

However, if part of the bedrock of Christian belief is that 'the judge of the earth will do what is right' (Genesis 18:25), then not only can we have confidence that whatever God does judicially in this world is proper, but that adjustments for any perceived deficiencies will be made in the final judgement.

Provisional and final judgement

It is the doctrine of future judgement which will be impeccably conducted by the all-knowing, all-wise, all-just God, which goes a long way towards countering the charge that God's action towards the Canaanites (and others) is unfair. It is this prospect of future judgement which alone satisfies those deeds which 'cry out to heaven' for a hell, for only God can provide this and, if he is to be true to himself, must provide it.

Kidner helpfully underscores the importance of this teaching if we are to have a biblical appreciation of the conquest events. He writes that it is; 'the final judgement which will correct the rough justice of history'. He goes on to write:

> This was a strong theme of our Lord's teaching. 'It shall be more tolerable on the day of judgement for Tyre and Sidon than for you; more tolerable ... for the land of Sodom than for you.... the men of Nineveh will rise at the judgement of this generation and condemn it ...' (Matthew 11:22, 24; 12:41). It answers the concern for fair dealing which was already implied by the prayers of Old Testament intercessors against God's sweeping temporal judgements, and by more than one protest against his heavy-handed agents, who furthered the disaster when he was angry but a little (Zechariah 1:15). 'The Judge of all the earth' must do right: this was crystal-clear in Abraham's day, though it emerged only by degrees that the present age just opens a man's account, and the date of his death has little bearing on the 'everlasting life' or the 'shame and everlasting contempt', which are the ultimates (Daniel 12.2).[103]

This future (eschatological) dimension is integral to any fully orbed Christian 'defence of the ways of God in the face of evil' (what theologians call 'theodicy'). This includes a proper understanding and appreciation of the conquest commands and narratives. They stand at just one point in God's dealings with the world and his people, demonstrating his holy anger and holy love simultaneously. There are other points along the way where we see that same revelation, supremely at the cross where God's justice and love meet upon the thorn-laden brow of Jesus. But what we also see in the conquest story is, as it were, a reflective echo backwards in time of the final judgement which will take place at the end of time. The judgement in time is provisional, and to some extent 'rough', the final judgement will be perfect and precise.

D. A. Carson's summarises the Christian's position well:
> The prospect of the End, of a consummated kingdom, of the ultimate division between heaven and hell, are all enormously important aspects of all Christian thought about evil and suffering. We serve a just God, and at the end, not only will justice be done, but it will be seen to be done.[104]

10. The Bible, the whole Bible and nothing but the Bible (and the Cross)

There are two assumptions undergirding the defence against the charge that in the case of the Canaanites God instigated genocide which now need to be made explicit.

The entire Scripture is God's Word

The first is the belief in *tota Scriptura* (the entirety of Scripture).

This is the acknowledgement of the total unity and authority of Scripture. The biblical texts together form the big picture (metanarrative) which make up the Christian worldview. This means that the Canaanite conquest has to be placed within this wider framework for us to understand its full meaning and significance. Within the context of the narratives themselves, as part of the bigger unfolding story of God's dealings with his people Israel and his intended blessings for the world, we see that God's character provides sufficient grounds for the Israelites to carry out his commands to exact judicial punishment upon the Canaanite people. Within the larger biblical picture which takes us into the New Testament, we have seen that such judgement is not an extraordinary 'blip' but part of God's ongoing judgement in the world as well as an anticipation of the final judgement to come. Whilst there is the operation of God's holiness against sin, we also see the richer operation of God's grace in mercy.

Interwoven into the events are also the promises of God's salvation as expressed, for example, in Genesis 12 and 15 that a land will be given to Abraham's descendants from which a 'seed' will come who will be the Saviour of all peoples (Galatians 3:16ff). Therefore, a necessary condition for this is that the corrupt and corrupting Canaanites be removed. If the last judgement is to be taken seriously, together with other temporal expressions of God's wrath (Romans 1:18ff; Revelation 6, 14 etc.), then there can be no substantial objection that the means used to eject the Canaanites was immoral any more than any judicial capital punishment is immoral given that the judgement is warranted.

The entire Scripture is enough for what we need

The second assumption is that of *sola Scriptura* (the sufficiency of Scripture).

The Bible is not only the controlling narrative of the Christian worldview, but its specific statements about God, (what Professor Paul Helm calls, 'credal one-liners'[105]) as well as God's commands and actions, understood within their various contexts (literary, historic, canonical), together make up the content of the Christian faith. This means that the Bible is the place Christians turn to in order to discover what is considered to be good and what are to be our moral norms as God determines them.

Bearing this in mind there are therefore no grounds for taking what is presented as a unique situation regarding the conquest of Canaan and extending it to any alleged modern equivalent of a 'holy war'. In the New Testament such *herem* language is transposed into that which is primarily spiritual, not only as Christians 'fight' against principalities and powers but also as they pursue personal holiness. Whatever hyperbole there may be, the kind of language originally used to call the people of Israel not to tolerate evil in the land and radically remove it as embodied in its residents, is reapplied by Jesus to his followers to take radical steps to remove evil from their own lives: 'If your right hand causes you to sin, cut it off and throw it away. It is better for you to lose one part of your body than for your whole body to go into hell'.[106] If we take this as an *a fortiori* argument (from the lesser to the greater) there may be a case for saying that if such uncompromising steps have to be taken in the life of a Christian in 'fighting the good fight' in order to avoid a dreadful judgement to come, then projecting this principle backwards to a different time and different situation, equivalent steps had to be taken by God's people under God's express command in the occupation of the land of Canaan:

> ...the ancient practice of *herem*, or 'holy war', which was meant to rid Israel of ungodly people and practices, has been replaced by the concept of spiritual warfare, in which Christians are permanently engaged... To put it briefly, what Israel did externally in the context of a nation state, Christians do internally as a people chosen by God from every state and nation. The principles are the same but the way they are

> worked out is different, which is why Paul is able
> to say that the law of Israel has been superseded
> by the Gospel of Jesus Christ.[107]

Furthermore, given that the Old Testament looks forward to the New and the Old is to be read in the light of this fuller revelation, there is one event which above all others provides a lens through which we are to gain a deeper understanding of the Conquest, namely, that of the cross of Christ.

Back to the Cross

We might think of Jesus' work on the Cross as 'fulfilling' the Scripture of the Canaanite conquest in the following way:

In the Bible Jesus is presented as God's Servant (Isaiah 42:1-7), and so the True Israel (cf. Isaiah 41:3), the True Vine that Israel was meant to be (John 15:1-8 cf. Isaiah 5:1-7) such that all that are united to him are themselves 'the true Israel' (cf. Galatians 6:16). On the cross, as the Suffering Servant (Isaiah 42; 52:13-53:12), Jesus did the work of defeating evil and liberating his people from sin, paralleling the defeat of evil and the liberation of the land of Canaan (Colossians 2:13-15). The conquest which Israel only partially and temporarily achieved was recapitulated and transcended by the True Israel—Jesus.

But we may go further and see in Jesus as the sin-bearing substitute the embodiment of the Canaanites in their rebellion and degeneracy.[108] We may recall the Apostle Paul's breath-taking statement that, 'God made him who had no sin to be sin for us, so that in him we might become the righteousness of God'.[109] It was this doctrine which no doubt lay behind Martin Luther's equally shocking statement: 'Jesus became the greatest liar, perjurer, thief, adulterer and murderer that mankind has ever known—not because he committed these sins but because he was actually made sin for us.' In the same vein could we not reverently say that Jesus became the 'greatest Canaanite that mankind has ever known'? The wrath of God which fell upon the Canaanites through the instrument of Israel fell upon all such 'Canaanites' through the instrument of the Cross. As Jesus became the True Israel, he became the 'true Canaan' as he suffered the holy anger against all acts of unrighteousness, even those of such a vile nature as perpetrated by the Canaanites and all those who have followed in their footsteps ever since. 'Jesus becomes the person whom God destroys so that in him we become the people God defends.'[110]

As God's wrath and mercy were shown in the conquest, albeit in broken form in a broken world, they are perfectly displayed and transcended in the great conquest of the Cross and will be fully consummated on the Final Day with the return of Christ.

It is also the Cross of Christ which puts paid to the false antithesis often posed between the so-called 'God of the Old Testament' and the 'God of the New' as Sproul rightly reminds us:

> The false conflict between the two testaments may be seen in the most brutal act of divine vengeance ever recorded in Scripture. It is not found in the Old Testament but in the New Testament. The most violent expression of God's wrath and justice is seen in the Cross. If ever a person had room to complain of injustice, it was Jesus. He was the only innocent man to be punished by God. If we stagger at the wrath of God, let us stagger at the Cross. Here is where

our astonishment should be focused. If we have cause for moral outrage, let it be directed at Golgotha ...The Cross was at once the most horrible and the most beautiful example of God's wrath. It was the most just and the most gracious act in history. God would have been more than unjust. He would have been diabolical to punish Jesus if Jesus had not first willingly taken on Himself the sins of the world. Once Christ had done that, once He volunteered to be the Lamb of God, laden with our sins, then he became the most grotesque and vile things on this planet. With the concentrated load of sin he carried, He became utterly repugnant to the Father. God poured out His wrath on this obscene thing. God made Christ accursed for the sin he bore. Herein was God's holy justice manifest. Yet it was done for us.[III]

The corrective lens of the Cross through which all God's mysterious purposes of salvation and judgement are to be viewed (including the conquest of Canaan) has been eloquently summarised by P. T. Forsyth:

If the greatest act in the world, and the greatest crime there; became by the moral, holy victory of the Son of God, the source of not only endless blessing to man, but perfect satisfaction and delight to a holy God, then there is no crime, no war, which is outside his control or impossible for his purpose. There is none that should destroy the Christian faith which has as its object, source and sustenance that cross and its victory, in which the prince of this world has in principle been judged and doomed for ever. In the Cross of Christ we learn the faith that things not willed by God are yet worked up by God. In a

> divine irony, man's greatest crime turns God's greatest boon. The riddle is insoluble but the fact sure.[112]

One final comment from Vanhoozer which itself is a clear summary of the position of this book:

> The divine command (to a specific generation of Israelites) to kill the Canaanites, when properly interpreted in its redemptive-historical context and viewed in the shadow of the cross, no more contradicts Jesus' teaching (to his disciples, playing a different scene in the drama of redemption) than God's holiness contradicts God's love. The 'answer' is simplicity itself: divine simplicity, namely, the idea that the divine attributes do not name 'parts' of God but offer a perspective on the whole of God's being.[113]

God is white hot holy love. This was shown at a special, unique moment in salvation-history in the entry of God's people into the land of Promise; it was shown supremely in the salvation of the world on the Cross of Calvary, and will be consummated at the return of Christ and the wedding supper of the Lamb.

Notes

1 C.S. Lewis, *God in the Dock: Essays on Theology* (Fount, Collins, 1979), p.100

2 Richard Dawkins, *The God Delusion* (Black Swan, 2007), p.31

3 Ibid., p.280

4 Charles Templeton, *Farewell to God: My Reasons for Rejecting the Christian Faith* (McClelland & Stewart, 2000) p.71

5 http://www.goodreads.com/quotes/show/25755

6 See Christopher Hitchens, *God is Not Great: How Religion Poisons Everything* (Atlantic Books, 2007)

7 D.A. Carson, *How Long O Lord? Reflections on Suffering and Evil* (Inter Varsity Press, 1990), pp.94-95

8 http://www.patheos.com/blogs/peterenns/2013/10/the-best-way-of-getting-out-of-the-whole-canaanite-genocide-thing-and-it-comes-right-from-the-bible-but-you-may-not-like-it

9 http://www.bethinking.org/bible/old-testament-mass-killings

10 C.S. Cowles, 'Case for Radical Discontinuity' in *Show Them No Mercy* (Zondervan, 20013) p.38 and p.148

11 Marcion developed a teaching around AD144 that the God of the Old Testament (whom he called the Demiurge) was the creator of the material universe and was to be equated with the jealous tribal deity of Israel which stood in contrast to the God of universal compassion that Jesus proclaimed.

12 Paul Copan, *Is God a Moral Monster? Making Sense of the Old Testament God* (Grand Rapids: Baker, 2011), p.171

[13] Ibid., pp.175-176

[14] Ibid., p.181; 178

[15] Clay Jones, 'We don't hate sin so we don't understand what happened to the Canaanites' in *Philosophia Christi* Vol 11, No 1, 2009

[16] Carson, op. cit., p.106

[17] John Bright, *The Authority of the Old Testament*, SCM, (1967), p 77f. The importance of being ruled by the biblical text, rather than our own moral intuitions about what God must do, has recently been put forward by Kevin J Vanhoozer: 'Why did Jesus himself not find Deuteronomy's depiction of God abhorrent? Probably because he was not working with the concept of "morally perfect being". I find it interesting that Rauser and Morriston treat their own moral intuitions about what a perfect being must do as more reliable (dare I say inerrant?) than the biblical text. As Christians, they should know that the wisdom of the world is the foolishness of God.' Kevin J Vanhoozer, 'Augustinian Inerrancy: Literal Meaning, Literal Truth, And Literal Interpretation in the Economy of biblical Discourse', in *Five Views of biblical Inerrancy* ed. J Merrick (Zondervan, 2013), p.232

[18] https://www.youtube.com/watch?v=V7B5jokJsqk

[19] The role of background beliefs held by people in a society is helpfully set out by Barry Barnes: 'For most people, whatever their way of life, the beliefs they accept and utilize are held unselfconsciously, and are rarely reflected upon. Moreover, when reflection does occur, it tends to depict these beliefs as natural representations of 'how things are'. Critical analytical examination of beliefs, their origin, functions, and claims to validity, is the province of specialised, academic roles in modern societies, and is a phenomenon of little general significance. The 'western layman' lives in a taken-for-granted world: solid, objective intelligible; on the whole he thinks with his beliefs, but not about them.' Barry Barnes, *Scientific Knowledge a Sociological Theory* (London: Routledge and Kegan Paul, 1974).

[20] David L. Wolfe, *Epistemology* (Inter Varsity Press, Grove, 1982), p. 51

[21] An ad hominem argument literally means you attack the man not his ideas, for example, 'You would say that wouldn't you because you are a white Anglo-Saxon protestant male!' Rational argument is bypassed.

[22] Cited by Os Guinness in *Unspeakable: Facing up to the Challenge of Evil* (Harper One, 2006), p 39

[23] *Show Them No Mercy* pp.15-17

[24] https://www.youtube.com/watch?v=V7B5jokJsqk

[25] The writer wisely cautions that whatever arguments might be adduced to square divine justice, goodness and holiness with the command to slaughter the Canaanites in tandem with reference to the inscrutability of divine justice, it will provoke dismay unless 'it incorporates at its heart God's sorrowful accommodation'. S. N. Williams, 'Could God have Commanded the Slaughter of the Canaanites?', *Tyndale Bulletin* 63.2 (2012), pp 173-175

[26] Ibid., p.232

[27] Revelation 21:4

[28] Daniel L. Gard, 'The Case of Eschatological Continuity' in *Show them No Mercy,* p.140

[29] By speaking of God as 'good' we do not mean that it is an attribute of God, like his omniscience, but we are referring to his nature. This is the way Stephen Charnock expresses it, 'Goodness is not a quality in him, but a nature; not a habit added to his essence, but his essence itself; he is not first God, and then afterwards is good; but he is good as he is God, his essence, being one and the same, is formally and equally God and good.' In *Discourse Upon the Existence and Attributes of God* (London: Bohn, 1853), pp.542-43.

[30] This is why priority has to be given to exegesis, understanding what the text does say and means in its own terms, especially regarding the character of God, rather than having our own notions of God to in effect determine what we think the Bible should say and mean. 'What we find therefore in the Old Testament and in Paul is what God defines as "right" in terms of himself. There is no other standard to consult than his own infinitely worthy being.' John Piper, *The Future of Justification* (Inter Varsity Press, 2008), p.63

[31] By epistemological warrants we mean that someone is entitled to believe certain things to be true which they may not fully understand and which have not been discovered through reason but which have a good grounding, e.g. divine revelation.

[32] This is a phrase owed to D. A. Carson in another context which conveys the idea that there are certain unchangeable beliefs which are not open to negotiation and so alteration, 'Factors Determining Current Hermeneutical Debate' in *Biblical Interpretation and the Church—Text and Context* (ed. D. A. Carson, Paternoster, 1984), p.13

[33] This is an idea which is thoroughly explored to great effect by Richard Bauckham in *Jesus and the God of Israel*, (Paternoster Press, 2008).

[34] I owe this insight to Dr Dale Ralph Davies

[35] Ibid., p.8

36 It is important to note how the text goes on to express God's command to rid the land of the Canaanites because of their idolatry and that Yahweh is a jealous God, vv.10-17. This is a basic revelation of God, as John Calvin writes: 'Here we may observe, first, that his eternity and self-existence are declared by his magnificent name twice repeated; and, secondly, that in the enumeration of his perfections, he is described not as he is in himself, but in relation to us, in order that our acknowledgment of him may be a more vivid actual impression than empty visionary speculation. Moreover, the perfections that are enumerated are just those we saw shining in the heavens, and on earth—compassion, goodness, mercy, justice, judgement, and truth. For the power and energy are comprehended under the name Jehovah.' *Institutes of the Christian Religion*, I. 10.2 (Translated by Henry Beveridge. Reprint. Peabody, MA: Hendrickson, 2008). This revelation is crucial for understanding the character of God and therefore the question of warrants to trust and obey him, for as Calvin says these are a 'vivid actual impression' of God rather than an 'empty visionary speculation'.

37 R. C. Sproul, *The Holiness of God* (Tyndale House, Illinois, 1998), p. 120

38 When we consider Joshua, we must foreground theologically the canonical context and insist that, if God could have commanded the slaughter of the Canaanites, it could only have been with the heaviest of hearts, channelling the human impulse to kill, an impulse which is the most dreadful sign and manifestation of disorder and fall. It is not thus that God would gladly express or reveal the glory of his nature. This theological interpretation is not advertised in the book of Joshua, but the book of Joshua makes fatal reading unless it is read as part of the canon of Scripture, with emphasis on the first nine chapters of its first book.' S. N Williams, op. cit., p.175

[39] Yahweh acts 'within the framework of divine perfection, justice, fidelity, integrity, righteousness, and consistency', so writes Daniel Block, 'How can we bless YHWH? Wrestling with Divine violence in Deuteronomy', *Wrestling with the violence of God : soundings in the Old Testament* eds. M. Daniel Carrol R and J Blair Wilgus, (Winona Lake, Indiana: Eisenbrauns, 2015) p.36

[40] Greg Koukl, https://bible.org/article/canaanites-genocide-or-judgement. We may also note that this is an essential strand of Paul's argument in Romans 9 in his defence of the doctrine of election, which is grounded in God's grace. He concludes, 'Therefore God has mercy on whom he wants to have mercy, and he hardens whom he wants to harden. One of you will say to me: "Then why does God still blame us? For who resists his will?" But who are you, O man, to talk back to God? Shall what is formed say to him who formed it, "Why did you make me like this?" Does not the potter have the right to make out of the same lump of clay some pottery for noble purposes and some for common use?' (Romans 9:18-21).

[41] Basil Mitchell, 'Theology and Falsification', in *New Essays in Philosophical Theology* (ed. Flew and McIntyre, 1955), pp.103-4

[42] To some extent almost all language about God is 'picture language'—metaphorical. Traditionally both Jews and Christians have taken such revelation language to be analogical. Metaphors are used which convey some truth or other about the nature and character of God; the trick is deciding which elements are applicable and which aren't. 'The reason that nearly all the language we use about God is analogical in this way is because our language is designed to describe our experience of the created order and, with the one exception of the human nature of God the Son, God is not a creature. It follows that we either have to use language analogically when we refer to God or say nothing at all.' Martin Davie 'On the Use of Pronouns' — http://anglicanmainstream.org/on-the-use-of-pronouns/

[43] See J.I. Packer, 'The Jealous God', in *Knowing God*, pp 189-198 (Hodder, 1993)

[44] C H Dodd, *The Epistle to the Romans*, (Fontana, 1959)

[45] Leon Morris, *The Apostolic preaching of the Cross*, (Tyndale Press, 1960).

[46] Indeed this is Isaiah's language, cf. 28:21

[47] Miroslav Volf, *Free of Charge: Giving and Forgiving in a Culture Stripped of Grace* (Grand Rapids: Zondervan, 2006), pp.138-9

[48] See D.A. Carson, *The Difficult Doctrine of the Love of God* (Inter varsity Press, 2000), p.80

[49] Ibid., p.81

[50] Ibid., p.81

[51] J.A.T Robinson, *Wrestling with Romans* (SCM, 1979), p.19

[52] B. B. Warfield, 'The Glory of Christ': cited in Carl Trueman, *The Wages of Spin* (Mentor, Christian Focus Publications, 2004), pp. 122-123

[53] Derek Kidner, *Hard Sayings: The Challenge of Old Testament Morals* (Inter Varsity Press, 1972), p.41

[54] Ibid., p.41

[55] John Stott and David L. Edwards, *Evangelical Essentials* (Inter Varsity Press, 1988), p.263

[56] Clay Jones, 'We don't hate sin so we don't understand what happened to the Canaanites' in *Philosophia Christi* Vol 11, No 1, 2009

[57] Ibid, p.57

[58] C Jones, 'Killing the Canaanites: A Response to the New Atheism's "Divine Genocide"' www.equip.org/articles/killing-the-canaanites

[59] This might explain why God ordered the destruction of even domestic animals. 'No one would want to have animals around that were used to having sex with humans', Jones, p 66

[60] Ibid., p.61

[61] Ibid., footnote

[62] Ibid., p.62, footnote

[63] Ibid, p.53

[64] Daniel L. Gard—response to Eugene Merrill in, *Show them no Mercy—Four Views on God and the Canaanite Genocide* (Ed Stanley N. Gundry, Zondervan, 2003), p.104

[65] Instead, the Israelites worshiped the Canaanites' gods and "did evil" (Judges 10:6; 1 Kings 14:22; 2 Kings 17:10). They had "male shrine prostitutes" (1 Kings 14:22), committed acts of "lewdness," adultery, and incest (Jeremiah 5:7; 29:23; Hosea 4:13–14; Ezekiel 22:10–11; Amos 2:7), and even Solomon set up an altar to Molech (1 Kings 11:5, 7–8). But instead of repenting when things went badly, they concluded that their misfortune was because they stopped burning incense to "the Queen of Heaven," Inanna/Ishtar (Jeremiah 44:18). So the Lord said that Israel became "like Sodom to me" (Jeremiah 23:14). In short, Israel was Canaanised.' Jones in, Killing the Canaanites: A Response to the New Atheism's "Divine Genocide" Claims, op. cit.

[66] Tremper Longman III, 'A Case for Spiritual Continuity' in *Show Them No Mercy*, p.163

Notes

67 Understanding the *HEREM*'. J. P. U. Lilley, *Tyndale Bulletin,* 1993, 44.1, pp.169-177, cf P. C. Craigie, *The Problem of War in the Old Testament* (Grand Rapids, Eerdmans 1978) p.49

68 'See, I am sending an angel ahead of you to guard you along the way and to bring you to the place I have prepared. Pay attention to him and listen to what he says. Do not rebel against him; he will not forgive your rebellion, since my Name is in him. If you listen carefully to what he says and do all that I say, I will be an enemy to your enemies and will oppose those who oppose you. My angel will go ahead of you and bring you into the land of the Amorites, Hittites, Perizzites, Canaanites, Hivites and Jebusites, and I will wipe them out. Do not bow down before their gods or worship them or follow their practices. You must demolish them and break their sacred stones to pieces. Worship the LORD your God, and his blessing will be on your food and water. I will take away sickness from among you, and none will miscarry or be barren in your land. I will give you a full life span.'

'I will send my terror ahead of you and throw into confusion every nation you encounter. I will make all your enemies turn their backs and run. I will send the hornet ahead of you to drive the Hivites, Canaanites and Hittites out of your way. But I will not drive them out in a single year, because the land would become desolate and the wild animals too numerous for you. Little by little I will drive them out before you, until you have increased enough to take possession of the land.'

'I will establish your borders from the Red Sea to the Mediterranean Sea, and from the desert to the Euphrates River. I will give into your hands the people who live in the land, and you will drive them out before you. Do not make a covenant with them or with their gods. Do not let them live in your land or they will cause you to sin against me, because the worship of their gods will certainly be a snare to you.'

69 Ibid., p.174

70 Ibid., p.174

[71] Longman, op. cit., p.164

[72] G. K. Beale, *The Morality of God in the Old Testament* (P & R Publishing, 2013), pp.10-11

[73] Ibid., p.11

[74] Christopher J. H. Wright, *The God I don't Understand: Reflections on Tough Questions of Faith* (Zondervan, 2008), p.90.

[75] Kevin J Vanhoozer, 'Augustinian Inerrancy: Literal Meaning, Literal Truth, And Literal Interpretation in the Economy of biblical Discourse', in *Five Views of biblical Inerrancy* ed. J Merrick (Zondervan, 2013), p.233, citing Daniel I. Block, *Deuteronomy*, The NIV Application Commentary (Zondervan, 2012), p.483

[76] Kidner, op. cit., p.41

[77] Kidner, op. cit., p.42

[78] https://www.youtube.com/watch?v=V7B5jokJsqk

[79] Greg Koukl, https://bible.org/article/canaanites-genocide-or-judgement p.

[80] See Paul Copan, *Is God a Moral Monster?*, p.179

[81] Paul Coulter, 'Killing in the Old Testament', http://www.bethinking.org/bible/old-testament-mass-killings, p.6 The same argument is adopted by P. J. Williams https://www.youtube.com/watch?v=V7B5jokJsqk

[82] Coulter, op. cit.

[83] https://www.youtube.com/watch?v=9FGv9aOCcyU

[84] P. Copan, 'Yahweh Wars and the Canaanites—Divinely Mandated Genocide or Corporal Capital Punishment?' *Philosophia Christi* Vol. 11.1, 2009: 73-90

[85] Cited by Copan, p.83. John Allister in his consideration of the annihilation of the Amalekites writes, 'So the command in 1 Samuel 15:3 looks a lot less like genocide, and a lot more like "If anyone—man, woman, child, whoever—doesn't take the chance to give up their identity as Amalekites and therefore also their opposition to Israel, then kill them. And make sure that you don't profit from doing it."'. He goes on to question the application of the term genocide in that 'This is about breaking and destroying the identity of Amalek as a nation, so they as a nation cannot continue to oppose God's plan to bless the world. It isn't about hatred of individuals, or about killing those individuals, unless they want to keep on being Amalekites and to keep on fighting against God's plan. It is then questionable whether it is genocide in the modern sense. It doesn't involve dehumanisation of the ethnic group; it doesn't seem to involve lack of mercy or love. But it is destroying the identity of a nation that has set itself against God and his plan to bless the world, and all who cling to that identity.' John Allister, 'The Amalekite Genocide', *Churchman*, 2010, 124/3 pp.224-225. This could equally be applied to the Canaanite conquest.

[86] D. A. Carson, *How Long O Lord* pp.47-48

[87] Coulter, op. cit., p.8

[88] Coulter, op. cit., p.9

[89] Longman, op. cit., p.185

[90] An historian who witnessed the destruction of Jerusalem and the desecration of the Temple after the siege of four years, described the horror. The famine was so severe that mothers ate their children. Rival groups within the city slaughtered one another and desecrated the Temple long before the Roman troops breached the walls of the city. The entire populace was either slaughtered or sold into slavery and the city was burned and razed to the ground.' D. A. Carson, *God with Us—Themes from Matthew* (Wipf and Stock, 1995), p.142

[91] See Melvin Tinker, *Why Do Bad Things Happen to Good People?* (Christian Focus, 1997) also Melvin Tinker, *Intended for Good—the Providence of God* (Inter Varsity Press, 2012).

[92] Kidner, op. cit., p.43

[93] Norman Angell, *The Great Illusion: A study of the Relations of Military Power to National Advantage* (Bottom of the Hill Publications, 2012), p.103

[94] Ibid., pp.119-120

[95] Albert Martin, *The Last Crusade: The Church of England in the First World War* (Duke University Press, 1974), p.66

[96] P. T Forsyth, *The Justification of God, Lectures for War-Time on a Christian Theodicy* (Wipf and Stock, 1999), pp.22- 23

[97] Richard Bauckham, *The Theology of the Book of Revelation* (CUP, 1993) pp.80-84

[98] Referred to by Tremper Longman, op. cit., p.185, Meredith Kline, *The Structure of biblical Authority* (Grand Rapids: Eerdmans, 1972).

[99] Longman, op. cit., p.185

[100] This account is taken from A. R. Eckardt, 'The Recantation of the Covenant?' in A. H. Rosenfeld and I. Greenberg, eds., *Confronting the Holocaust: The Impact of Elie Wiesel* (Bloomington: Indiana University Press, 1978) p.163

[101] Cited by Os Guinness in *Unspeakable—Facing Up to Evil in an Age of Genocide and Terror* (Harper Collins, 2005), p.217

[102] The implications of demanding that God acts now to deal with injustice are not often carefully considered for if they were, we may be a little more reluctant to make such a demand. This has been eloquently put by Dorothy L. Sayers, '"Why doesn't God smite this dictator dead?" is a question a little remote from us. Why, madam did he not strike you dumb and imbecile before you uttered that baseless and unkind slander the day before yesterday? Or me, before I behaved with such a cruel lack of consideration to that well meaning friend? And why sir, did he not cause your hand to rot off at the wrist before you signed your name to that dirty bit of financial trickery? You did not quite mean that? But why not? Your misdeeds and mine are none the less repellent because our opportunities for doing damage are less spectacular than those of some other people. Do you suggest that your doings and mine are too trivial for God to bother about? That cuts both ways; for in that case, it would make precious little difference to his creation if he wiped us both out tomorrow.' Dorothy L Sayers 'The Triumph of Easter' *Creed or Chaos* (Methuen 1954). For a more general consideration of the relationship between God's sovereignty and evil see, Melvin Tinker, 'The Suffering of Man and the Sovereignty of God—An Examination of the Relationship between the Problem of Evil and the Purposes of God', *Churchman* 109/1 1995.

[103] Kidner, op. cit., pp.43-44

[104] Carson, op. cit., p.147

[105] Paul Helm, *Faith, Form and Fashion—Classical Reformed Theology and Its Postmodern Critics* (Cascade Books, 2014), pp.91-93

[106] Matthew 5:30

[107] Gerald Bray, *God is Love—A biblical and Systematic Theology*, (Crossway, 2012), p.42

[108] John Allister draws a similar parallel with regards to Amalek, op. cit., p.225

[109] 2 Corinthians 5:21

[110] Allister, op. cit., p.226

[111] Sproul, op. cit., pp.121-122

[112] P. T. Forsyth, *The Justification of God*, p.155

[113] Vanhoozer, op. cit., p.234

FROM MOUNTAINS

Snowdon Range, North Wales

TO LAKES

Trefeglwys, Mid Wales

TO THE SEA

Three Cliffs Bay, Gower, South Wales

CW00685685

A BRIEF TIMELINE OF WELSH HISTORY

4,000 BC Farming is introduced into Wales

2,000 BC Bronze is introduced into Wales

1,000 BC Hill forts built during the Iron Age

600 BC The Celts settle in Wales

50 AD The Romans begin the conquest of Wales

78 AD The Romans conquered Wales

407 The Roman army leaves Britain. Afterwards Wales splits into separate kingdoms.

856 Rhodri Mawr defeats the Danes

1040 First Prince of Wales, Gruffydd ap Llywelyn secured borders

1063 English invaded: Gruffydd ap Llywelyn killed

1066 Normand invaded: King Harold of England killed.

1215 Magna Carta signed

1255 Llewellyn becomes king of Gwynedd

1267 Henry III of England makes the Treaty of Montgomery with Llewellyn

1277 Llewellyn is forced to submit to the English king Edward I

1282 The Welsh rebel

1283 The rebellion is crushed

1294 The Welsh rebel again

1295 The rebellion is crushed

1301 Edward makes his son, also called Edward, Prince of Wales

1400 Owain Glyndwr leads another rebellion

1413 The rebellion ends

1485 Henry Tudor lands at Milford Haven

1536 The Act of Union reforms Welsh government

1563 Bible published in Welsh Language

1642 During the Civil War Wales supports the king

1647 Harlech Castle falls to parliamentary forces

1750 The Industrial Revolution begins to transform Wales

1800 First of great Welsh canals built

1839 The Rebecca Riots occurred, toll gate destroyed in protest against high fees

1850's Coal fields in South Wales developed

1900-03 Strike at Penrhyn Quarry; longest labour dispute in history; 3000 workers walked out

1913 Explosion at Senghenydd's pit killed 439 miners

1916 Lloyd George first Welshman to become British prime minister

1955 Cardiff became capital of Wales

1966 Slag pile collapsed at school in Aberfan, 144 children and teachers killed

1969 Investiture of Charles as Prince of Wales

1984 Year-long miner's strike virtually ended coal industry in the country

1999 The Welsh Assembly opens

2005 Charles, Prince of Wales married Camilla Parker Bowles

2008 Tower Colliery, last deep mine in Wales closed

2011 Prince William of Wales married Catherine Middleton

Welcome to "Around Wales Route 650"

The Route (shown dotted red on the map) starts and finishes in Cardiff, the capital of Wales and follows, in an anti-clockwise direction, the Wales - England border (including a short length of highway in England), the main coastal strips of North, West and South Wales.

However, the Route can be joined at any point depending on your arrival in Wales be it by air, sea, road or rail. The total length of the route, including those shown around scenic areas is some 650 miles.

Two major highways traverse east - west; the A55 Expressway in the north from the border to Holyhead in the west and the M4 Motorway in the south which extends westwards, again from the border, to beyond Swansea.

There are no 'high-speed road links' running north-south but a large network of various class of road exists across the country. Some of the major ones are shown in white on the main map. Wales has many interesting and picturesque locations inland and routes to some of these, which are not too far off the Around Wales Route 650, are shown in orange.

ITINERARIES

The picturesque Coastal route allows several ways of plotting your itinerary. The 6 day tour lays out a route, splitting each day into manageable distances and taking in some of the major highlights. The other 4 itineraries, Anglesey, Snowdonia, South Pembrokeshire and the Gower Peninsula have been drawn up for those with a specific interest, whether it be sea scape, mountains, National Parks or designated Areas of Outstanding Natural Beauty and so will take additional time to explore.

DAY 1 - Cardiff - Newtown approx 109mls

DAY 2 - Newtown - LLandudno approx 92mls

DAY 3 - Llandudno - Barmouth approx 83mls

DAY 4 - Barmouth - Fishguard. approx 99mls

DAY 5 - Fishguard - Swansea. approx 95mls

DAY 6 - Swansea - Cardiff. approx 52mls

INSET MAPS

ANGLESEY - page 28

SNOWDONIA - page 31

SOUTH PEMBROKESHIRE - page 37

GOWER PENINSULA - page 38

CARDIFF was granted city status in 1905 and recognised as the capital of Wales in 1955. It is Wales' largest city and the eleventh-largest city in the UK. A significant tourist centre and the most popular visitor destination in Wales.

The Romans invaded Wales about 50 AD and built a fort on the site of Cardiff castle. When the Normans conquered Glamorgan Robert Fitz Hammon built a wooden castle within the walls of the old Roman fort which was rebuilt in stone in the early 12th century. The town grew up in the shadow of the castle. Owen Glendower burnt Cardiff down in 1404 but it was rebuilt quickly as the buildings were of wood and thatched roofs. During the 15th, 16th and 17th centuries it was a small thriving port town trading with France and the Channel Islands as well as other British ports. The town grew rapidly from the 1830s onwards with the building of a dock, and Cardiff became the main port for exports of coal from the valleys. Its status as a major town came when the site of the University College South Wales and Monmouthshire was chosen in 1893.

In 1877 a permanent military presence was established in the town with the completion of Maindy Barracks.

More on Cardiff page 24, 25 and 40.

Starting the journey we leave Cardiff & head eastwards to the A48 towards Newport >>

DAY 1 Cardiff to Newtown

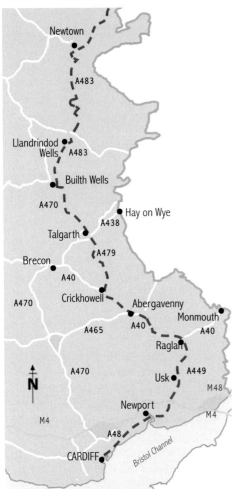

See pages 40 & 41 for larger scale road maps for Cardiff & Newport

NEWPORT

lies some 12 miles north-east of Cardiff and was granted city status in 2002. It lies on the River Usk close to its confluence with the Severn Estuary and is the third largest city in Wales.

Newport has long been a port and became the focus of coal exports from the eastern South Wales Valleys. Industry was expanding on the east side of the river with most of the population based on the west side which meant a 4 mile walk to cross the river by the town bridge. Although a ferry operated, due to the tide's changing times and its extreme rise and fall, it was impractical as a means of getting to work.

This prompted the construction of the now famous

Transporter Bridge as
a more economical
solution than tunnelling
under the river or the building of a bridge which would
allow the passage of the
tall ships of the era. The
bridge was opened in
1906. It is only one of six
Transporter Bridges still in
use.

You can get a different
perspective of Newport
from high up from the top of this Edwardian
Transporter Bridge.

Belle Vue Park's features are typical of a Victorian public park, including conservatories, pavilion, bandstand and rockeries. The Park also contains a number of rare specimens - the Himalayan Magnolias and Judas Trees blossom in May. In June and July the Tulip Tree produces its distinctive orange tulip-shaped flowers and Autumn brings glorious leaf colour including the clear yellow leaves of Ginko Biloba and the glorious crimson leaves of the Liquidambar. Entry to the Park is free but car parking charges apply.

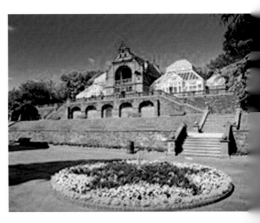

RAGLAN

stands at the crossing point of two Roman roads Gloucester to Usk and Chepstow to Abergavenny. Markets were held in the town from the mid 1300's and the market cross, a massive base on which a lamp post has been mounted, stands in the centre of the cross roads. The base of the cross formed the table on which bargains were struck.

In the late 14th century Raglan Castle was probably no more than a hill fort but early in the 15th it was greatly expanded. The castle ruins became neglected and were used as a quarry for those needing stone to repair their houses. Dressed stones can be seen in local farmhouses and cottages. The railway station buildings, following its closure in 1955, have been moved to St. Fagans Museum near Cardiff.

MONMOUTH

'Town on the Monnow", the historic county town of Monmouthshire where the River Monnow joins the River Wye, 2 miles from the border with England. The town was the site of a small Roman fort and became established after the Normans built a castle here. Its medieval stone gated bridge is the only one of its type remaining in Britain. The castle built in 1067 was the birthplace of King Henry V. By the end of the 18th century, the town had become a popular centre for visitors undertaking the "Wye Tour", an excursion by boat through the scenic Wye Valley

ABERGAVENNY

The market held on Tuesday, Friday and Saturday has long been the focus of trade through the town. Tradesmen sell all kinds of goods from locally grown produce to various crafted articles.

The once livestock market which had been active for over 150 years closed in 2013 and has now moved to Bryngwyn near Raglan.

CRICKHOWELL

Notable features include three churches, the seventeenth-century stone bridge over the River Usk (with its odd arches, twelve on one side, thirteen on the other, and its seat built into the walls, the 14th-century parish church of St Edmund, and the ruins of Crickhowell Castle on the green "tump" beside the A40 road.

Crickhowell's Market Hall (originally the Town Hall) on The Square dates from 1834, nowadays there are market stalls on the ground floor and a cafe on the first floor old courtroom. The stone building, raised on twin doric columns, is Grade II listed. The popular Green Man Festival is held here in August.

TALGARTH

Talgarth Church

This small market town has notable buildings including its 14th Century parish church and 13th Century Pele Tower located in the town centre.

Brecon Beacons National Park established in 1957 includes Pen y Fan, South Wales' highest mountain at 2907 ft. The Brecon Beacons are believed to be named after the ancient practice of lighting beacons on mountains to warn of attacks by invaders. They are used for training members of the UK armed forces and military reservists. One of the starting points for walkers up Pen y Fan is on the A470 known as Storey Arms, now an outdoor training centre.

HAY ON WYE

A small market town on the Welsh side of the Wales/England border is known for its bookshops and the venue for the annual Hay Literary Festival since 1988. The Festival draws thousands of visitors over a ten day period at the end of May / beginning of June, when big literary names from all over the world attend and give talks.

LLANDRINDOD WELLS

The Roman occupation of Britain provides the first evidence of spa waters in the area and still provides health-giving waters for visitors today. The Roman settlement at Castell Collen, just outside Llandrindod Wells is an important archaeological site. There are many regular attractions to cater for visitors including the Drama Festival Week at the beginning of May each year and the Victorian Festival at the end of August.

BRECON

Market town lies within the Brecon Beacons National Park. The Norman castle overlooking the town was built in the late 11th century. The town walls are built of cobble with four gatehouses. Today only fragments survive and these are protected as scheduled monuments. Saint Mary's church was built in 1510; the tower has eight bells which have been rung since 1750. It is a Grade II* listed building. Plough Lane Chapel in Lion Street is also a Grade II* listed building and dates back to 1841.

BUILTH WELLS

A pretty town and a delight to explore. The Wyeside Arts Centre on Castle Street was built as a market hall and Assembly Rooms during Builth's heyday as a Spa town. The first record of mineral waters at Builth comes from 1740, but it was not until further developments that Builth gained a reputation as a Spa town. Strand Hall, is a historic building, built in neoclassical style as a market hall with an exterior of red and yellow bricks. A Grade II listed pillar box in front of the Arts Centre dates back to the reign of George VI and on nearby West Street stands a pillar box which dates back to the reign of Queen Victoria. There are 43 listed buildings in Builth. The Groe is a life-sized sculpture of a black bull, a reminder of the origins of Builth Wells. The Royal Welsh Show, the largest agricultural show in the UK, is held here in July each year.

NEWTOWN

Was founded as a market town at the end of the 13th century. The town's connection with the textile industry was revived in the 20th century when businesswoman Laura Ashley established her home furnishing and clothing empire in the area. Nearby is a wealth of castles and country houses including Powys Castle & Gardens in Welshpool, Montgomery Castle, Dolforwyn Castle, Gregynog Hall & Gardens and Glansevern Hall & Gardens. A number of small local museums & galleries can be found in the centre of town. Newtown offers a variety of accommodation from hotels, lodges, cottages, b&b's and provides the ideal base to explore the surrounding area.

DAY 2 Newtown to Llandudno

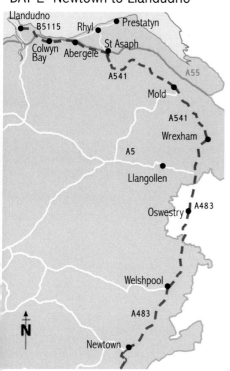

WELSHPOOL

A major attraction to Welshpool is the Monday Cattle Market, believed to be one of the largest one-day markets in the Europe. The Welshpool Carnival takes place in May.

The restored octagonal cockpit in the centre of the town is unusual being the only one in Wales on its original site.

The Welshpool & Llanfair Light Railway - a narrow gauge steam train, was originally built to take local people to market with their sheep and cattle, operates throughout the summer months between Easter and early October.

WREXHAM

The largest town in north Wales and an administrative, commercial, retail and educational centre. The Monday market is the largest in North Wales. It

is a very popular town to visit being a short drive away from a number of historical sites.

The nearby Pontcysyllte Aqueduct built over two hundred years ago to ferry raw materials and finished products in and out of the area. The arches reach a height of 200ft as they span the river. One can walk or ride in a canal boat along its entire length. In the summer months you can travel over the canal as you dine on a canal boat.

MOLD
Mold Castle, on Bailey Hill in the town is a motte-and-bailey castle erected around 1072. St Mary's Church, is an Anglican church and a Grade I listed building.

The Mold Food & Drink Festival is held each September. The food festival has a main event area on the edge of the town centre

LLANGOLLEN

One of the UNESCO World Heritage Sites with something for every visitor, is renowned for the surrounding hills and River Dee . Also for hosting the International Eisteddfod held annually in July when the town is awash with colour with the many contestants parading the streets in their national costumes.

RHUDDLAN Castle was erected by Edward I in 1277 but was not completed until 1282. It was King Edward I of England's temporarily residence, and his daughter, Elizabeth, is presumed to have been born there.

St ASAPH

This beautiful Cathedral was built around 1150 and enlarged to its present size by 1400. Its appearance, like a castle, is thought to be because it was built by Edward's castle builders.

BODELWYDDAN is well known for its "Marble Church". The Church was consecrated in 1860. It is open daily from 09:30 to 16:30 throughout the year except from Christmas Day until January 6th. St. Margaret's is one of Britain's finest Victorian Churches and its interior is decorated with a variety of marble.

COLWYN BAY Is a seaside resort with its long Promenade following the vast sweep from Old Colwyn to Penrhyn Bay.
Another attraction is the Welsh Mountain Zoo. with many rare and endangered species from around the world including snow leopards, red pandas, Sumatran tigers, chimpanzees and Californian sea lions.

LLANDUDNO

is a classic Victorian seaside resort with a pier, Punch and Judy show, Donkey Man and Alice in Wonderland. Travel up to summit of the Great Orme either by car, train or in a cable car where you'll be rewarded with incredible views of its surrounding mountains and coastal towns.

Great Orme

DAY 3 Llandudno to Barmouth

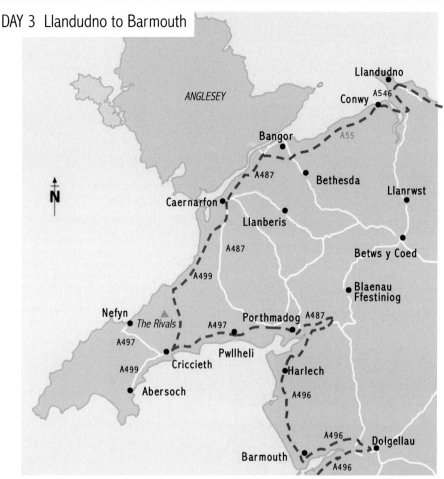

Llandudno

Conwy A546

ANGLESEY

A55

Bangor

A487

Bethesda

Llanrwst

Caernarfon

Llanberis

A487

Betws y Coed

A499

Blaenau
Ffestiniog

Nefyn

The Rivals

Porthmadog A487

A497

A497

Pwllheli

Criccieth

A499

Harlech

Abersoch

A496

A496

Dolgellau

Barmouth

A496

N

CONWY

The Quay offers a number of amenities where you can find the smallest house in Great Britain and also enjoy a refreshing drink outside or in a cosy quayside pub. Conwy also offers a whole host of places to eat and drink from fine dining restaurants, traditional pubs and snug cafes as well as a number of hotels and B&Bs.

Local boat tours are available at the Quay.

town with a mighty 13th-century castle and town alls. It is considered by UNESCO to be one of "the nest examples of late 13th century/early 14th cen-ury military architecture in Europe" and is classed as World Heritage site.

BANGOR, a university city, is the oldest city in Wales, one of the smallest cities in the United Kingdom and one of only six places classed as a city in Wales. Another claim to fame is that Bangor allegedly has the longest High Street in Wales and the United Kingdom.

Garth Pier is the second longest pier in Wales, and the ninth longest in the British Isles, at 1,500 feet in length. It was opened in 1893 and was a promenade pier. It was listed to be "the best in Britain of the older type of pier without a large pavilion at the landward end".

Bangor Cathedral - the Cathedral Church of St Deiniol is a Grade I Listed building and is set in a sloping oval churchyard. The site has been used for Christian worship since the sixth century but the present building dates from the twelfth century. It has a two-bay chancel, transepts, a crossing tower, a seven-bay nave and a tower at the west end. While the building itself is not the oldest, and certainly not the biggest, the bishopric of Bangor is one of the oldest in the UK.

CAERNARFON

A Royal town lying on the southern bank of the Menai Strait facing the Isle of Anglesey. The present castle building was constructed between 1283 and 1330. It is open to the public and includes the regimental museum of the Royal Welch Fusiliers. The investiture ceremony for Charles, Prince of Wales was held at the Castle in 1969.

Caernarfon town walls form a complete circuit around the old town, However, only a small section is accessible to the public. The town walls and castle are part of a World Heritage Site and claimed to be "the finest examples of late 13th century and early 14th century military architecture in Europe". The oldest public house in Caernarfon is the Black Boy Inn, which has stood inside the town walls since the 16th century, and many people claim to have seen ghosts within the building. The Old Market Hall is a Grade II listed building now a pub and music venue.

A market is held every Saturday throughout the year and also on Mondays in the Summer.

The statue of David Lloyd George in Castle Square was erected in 1921 when Lloyd George was Prime Minister. He is buried in Llanystymdwy near Porthmadog.

Caernarfon Airport is 4.5 miles to the south west. It has an aviation museum and offers pleasure flights.

In 1956, a large part of the Llŷn Peninsula was designated an Area of Outstanding Natural Beauty under the National Parks and Access to the Countryside Act 1949.

Nefyn

PORTHMADOG

The small Welsh coastal town developed in the 19th century after William Madocks built a sea wall, "the Cob", in 1810 to reclaim a large proportion of the beach from the sea for agricultural use. Porthmadog became a flourishing port for exporting slate as the rapidly expanding cities of England needed high quality roofing slate. The slate was transported to the new port by tramway from the quarries in Ffestiniog and Llanfrothen. However, since the decline of the slate industry Porthmadog has become a shopping centre and tourist destination. It is the terminus of the Ffestiniog Railway.

CRICCIETH

The building of the castle began in about 1230 and some 30 years later its size doubled with the addition of another wall and tower. In the early 13th Century Criccieth was little more than a church and a few houses beside the newly erected castle. In 1282 Edward I repaired the castle and built a chain of castles having conquered the land.

Portmeirion is a tourist village off the A487. It was designed and built by Sir Clough Williams-Ellis between 1925 and 1975 in the style of an Italian village, and is now owned by a charitable trust.

The Rivals

HARLECH

Harlech castle is a Grade I-listed medieval fortification. It was built by Edward I during his invasion of Wales between 1282 and 1289. During the 15th century Wars of the Roses, Harlech was held by the Lancastrians for seven years, before Yorkist troops forced its surrender in 1468. Following the outbreak of the English Civil War in 1642, the castle was held by forces loyal to Charles I, holding out until 1647 when it became the last fortification to surrender to the Parliamentary armies. It is now managed by Cadw, the Welsh Government's historic environment service, as a tourist attraction. Along with other castles in Wales UNESCO considers Harlech to be one of "the finest examples of late 13th century and early 14th century military architecture in Europe", and it is classed as a World Heritage site. It is built of local stone and concentric in design, featuring a massive gatehouse that probably once provided high-status accommodation for the castle constable and visiting dignitaries. The sea originally came much closer to Harlech and a water-gate and a long flight of steps leads down from the castle to the former shore, which allowed the castle to be resupplied by sea during sieges.

BARMOUTH

was once a shipbuilding town and more recently has become a seaside resort.

Buildings of interest include the medieval Ty Gwyn tower house, the 19th century Ty Crwn roundhouse prison and St John's Church.

William Wordsworth, a visitor to Barmouth in the 19th century, described it thus: "With a fine sea view in front, the mountains behind, the glorious estuary running eight miles inland, and Cadair Idris within compass of a day's walk, Barmouth can always hold its own against any rival".

The Barmouth Ferry sails from Barmouth to Penrhyn Point, where it connects with the narrow gauge Fairbourne Railway for the village of Fairbourne.

The busy harbour plays host to the annual Three Peaks yacht race.

Barmouth Bridge, which takes the Cambrian Line over the River Mawddach.

DAY 4 Barmouth to Fishguard

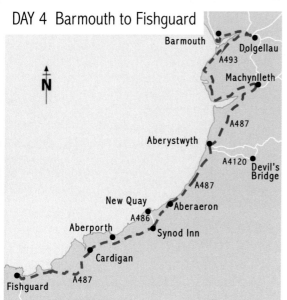

↑ N

Barmouth
Dolgellau
A493
Machynlleth
A487
Aberystwyth
A4120
Devil's Bridge
A487
New Quay
Aberaeron
A486
Aberporth
Synod Inn
Cardigan
Fishguard A487

ABERYSTWYTH

An ancient market town and holiday resort. The seafront boasts the oldest pier in Wales, built in 1864. The best vantage point is at the end of north beach's promenade atop Constitution Hill where you'll also find the world's largest Camera Obscura. This provides a bird's eye view of over 1000 square miles. The Camera Obscura is accessible via the Cliff Railway which is the longest cliff railway in Britain.

Aberystwyth is also a major Welsh educational centre with the establishment of a university college in 1872 and houses the National Library of Wales.

DEVIL'S BRIDGE

The village is best known for the bridge that spans the Afon Mynach. The bridge is unusual in that three separate bridges are coexistent, each one built upon the previous bridge: the earlier ones were not demolished

The unique Devils Bridge Falls is a world famous tourist attraction 12 miles east of Aberystwyth on the A4120.

ABERAERON

was developed from 1805 and the harbour operated as a port and supported a shipbuilding industry in the 19th century. Steam ships continued to visit the harbour until the 1920's; it is now a small half-tide harbour for recreational craft. The town is notable for the sale of honey and honey by-products.

An annual festival of Welsh ponies and cobs is held every August and the annual carnival takes place on August Bank Holiday Monday.

NEW QUAY

a beautiful fishing village with its picturesque harbour and sandy beach and trips from the harbour to see the bottle nose dolphins. Porpoise and Atlantic Grey seals can be viewed in the bay during certain times of the year. The New Quay Honey Farm, the largest bee farm in Wales is also a popular attraction. The annual Cardigan Bay Regatta which has been a feature in the area since before 1870 usually takes place in August.

FISHGUARD

consists of two parts, Lower Fishguard and the "Main Town".
The main town, with the Parish church and shops, which lies upon the hill, is joined by a steep and winding road to the south of Lower Fishguard. Lower Fishguard is believed to be the site of the original hamlet from which modern Fishguard has grown. It is in a deep valley where the River Gwaun flows and is a typical fishing village with a short tidal quay.

CARDIGAN

was developed around the Norman castle built in the late 11th/early 12th century and underwent restoration in 2014. The first
National Eisteddfod was held in the castle in 1176. The town became an important port in the 18th century, but declined by the early 20th century owing to its shallow harbour. Today Cardigan is a compact and busy town.

NEWPORT

a popular tourist destination was founded in about 1197 and was a busy port founded primarily on the growing medieval wool trade. Newport Castle is situated on a spur which overlooks the town and much of the surrounding countryside. Though in ruins since at least the 17th century, a house incorporating the castle walls is still inhabited. There is, in the town a significant mediaeval pottery kiln from the 15th century, believed to be the only intact example in Britain.

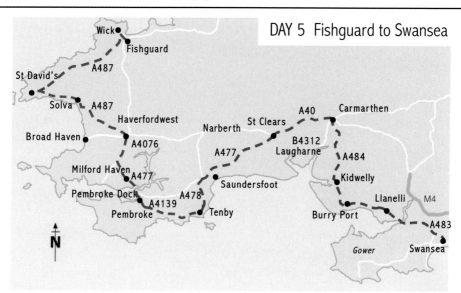

DAY 5 Fishguard to Swansea

ST DAVIDS

was given city status in the 16th century and is the UK's smallest city in terms of population and urban area. It is the final resting place of Saint David, Wales's patron saint, and named after him. In addition to the cathedral, interesting features include the 14th-century Tower Gate, the Celtic Old Cross and a number of art galleries.

SOLVA

boasts a bustling quay, a charming High Street with cafes, craft shops and galleries as well as easy access to beaches and walks both on the Pembrokeshire National Coast Path and inland.

Some of Pembrokeshire's Glorious Beaches

Broadhaven

St Brides Haven Beach

Dale

Marloes Sands

HAVERFORDWEST

Haverfordwest was established almost 1,000 years ago and in olden times was the second largest port in Wales. The centre of the town is dominated by the Western Cleddau that runs through the middle of the town and by the castle, built in about 1110. Situated within the Castle wall and previously the old prison governor's house is the town museum which houses exhibitions of art and local history and has artefacts relating to the town's past. On the bank of the river are the recently excavated and repaired ruins of an Augustinian Priory. They occupy a pleasant setting beside the river, a short walk from the town centre.

PEMBROKE

Pembroke Castle, a medieval castle, stands on a site that has been occupied at least since the Roman period. It is most famous for being the birthplace of Henry VII, the founder of the Tudor Dynasty and Britain's only Welsh king. Henry VII was King of England between 1485 and 1509.

It was designated a Grade I listed building in 1951, and later underwent major restoration.

The castle is the largest privately-owned castle in Wales and is open to the public.

MILFORD was founded in 1793 and takes its name from the natural harbour of **MILFORD HAVEN** which has been used as a port since. It was designed to a grid pattern, and originally intended to be a whaling centre, though by 1800 it was developing as a Royal Navy dockyard and remained as such until the dockyard was transferred to Pembroke in 1814. It then became a commercial dock. By 2010, the town's port had become the fourth largest in the United Kingdom in terms of tonnage, and continues its important role in the United Kingdom's energy sector with several oil refineries and one of the biggest LNG terminals in the world.

TENBY

A 13th century medieval walled town noted for its sandy beaches. The town walls include the Five Arches, built in the 16thC following fears of a second Spanish Armada, a barbican gatehouse, Museum and Art Gallery, a 15th Century Church St. Mary's. There are 372 listed buildings and other structures in and around Tenby. The Sunday Times rated Tenby's Castle Beach the best beach in the UK in 2019.
Boats sail from Tenby's harbour to the offshore monastic Caldey Island.

SAUNDERSFOOT

A large village and a popular holiday destinations. St Issells church lies in a dell to the north of Saundersfoot and is a Grade II* listed building.
The harbour was built for the export of anthracite coal from the many mines in the area, although coal was exported from the beach for centuries before this. The village grew up to serve the port which by 1837 had five jetties handling coal and iron ore and subsequently pig iron and firebricks from local sources. The industry finally faded away in the early years of the twentieth century.
Saundersfoot holds its annual charitable cheese festival and New Years Day swim every year which is sponsored by local businesses with more than 1,000 people taking part.

St CLEARS

The Priory Church of St Mary Magdalene was founded in around 1100 and is considered to have the best surviving Norman stone carving in Carmarthenshire. The stained-glass windows date from about 1929 in a Grade II listed building.

The Norman St Clears Castle was constructed in the 12th century and the town grew around it. The castle mound can still be seen.

LAUGHARNE

The home of Dylan Thomas from 1949 until his death in 1953. He is buried in Laugharne churchyard, his grave marked by a white cross. There are a number of landmarks namely the Boathouse, where he lived with his family from 1949 to 1953, and is now a museum; the parish church of St Martin and the 12th-century Castle.

NARBERTH

Was founded around a Welsh court, but later became a Norman stronghold. Attractions in the town include several art galleries, the Narberth Museum, the former town hall which still houses the cell where the leaders of the Rebecca Riots were imprisoned and a ruined castle. Narberth has a range of independent shops, and in 2014 The Guardian called it "not only a gastronomic hub for west Wales but also one of the liveliest, most likable little towns in the UK". Narberth Food Festival takes place on the fourth weekend of September every year and features celebrity chefs, cookery demonstrations, music, entertainment and children's activities. Narberth Civic Week is held during the last full week of July and includes a parade through the town to one of the churches, where a service is held to welcome the newly appointed Mayor. During Civic Week, there are various activities arranged for children, families and visitors to the town. The culmination of Civic Week is the annual Carnival Day Parade, a tradition dating back over 100 years. Narberth's Winter Carnival is held in December.

Laugharne Castle

Here two giant medieval stone towers stand guard over the remains of a magnificent Tudor mansion, all set in 19th century ornamental gardens.

CARMARTHEN

Claimed to be the oldest town in Wales but little remains of the original medieval castle. The old Gatehouse still dominates Nott Square. Castle House, within the old walls, is a museum and Tourist Information Centre. St Peter's is the largest parish church in the Diocese of St David's. Built of local red sandstone and grey shale it consists of a west tower, nave, chancel, south aisle and a Consistory Court. The tower contains eight bells.

Picton's monument was erected 1828 at the west end of the town to honour Lieutenant General Sir Thomas Picton, who had died at the Battle of Waterloo in 1815.

The foundation stone was laid on Monument Hill in 1847 and some 150 years later the top section was declared to be unsafe and was taken down. Four years later, the whole monument was rebuilt stone-by-stone on stronger foundations. There are many listed buildings in the town.

LLANELLI

Historically a mining town, Llanelli grew significantly in the 18th and 19th century with the mining of coal and later the tinplate industry and steelworks. With the decline in these, Llanelli is now a leisure and tourism destination, with many new developments such as the new Llanelli Scarlets rugby stadium, the Old Castle Works leisure village and a National Hunt racecourse at nearby Ffos Las.

Local attractions include the Millennium Coastal Path, the National Wetlands Centre, about 1-mile to the east of Llanelli. Llanelly House is one of Llanelli's most historic properties, an example of an early 18th-century Georgian town house, Parc Howard Museum set in the grounds of Parc Howard, St Elli's Parish Church is a Grade II* listed building.

Machynys Ponds, a Site of Special Scientific Interest notable for its dragonfly population, is 1 mile to the south of Llanelli.

KIDWELLY

was used as a location for the film Monty Python and the Holy Grail. The castle consists of a square inner bailey defended by four round towers, which overlook a semi-circular outer curtain wall on the landward side, with the massive gatehouse next to the river. The castle is relatively well-preserved, and is managed by Cadw.

BURRY PORT

lies on the Loughor estuary with its harbour looking south towards the picturesque Gower peninsula. In 1832 a harbour was built at Burry Port and the town developed around 1850. The harbour is now a marina for small leisure craft. The Pembrey Burrows sand dune and wetland system and the Cefn Sidan sands lie nearby. The town has a proud musical heritage. Burry Port is where Amelia Earhart landed as the first woman to fly across the Atlantic Ocean.

The National Botanic Garden of Wales is both a visitor attraction and a centre for botanical research and conservation, and features the world's largest single-span glasshouse.

It is situated off the A48 east of Carmarthen.

SWANSEA

was granted city status in 1969 to mark Prince Charles's investiture as the Prince of Wales. It is the second largest city in Wales. Within the city centre are: ruins of the castle, National Waterfront Museum, Glynn Vivian Art Gallery, Swansea Museum, Dylan Thomas Centre, and the Market, which is the largest covered market in Wales.

During the 19th-century industrial heyday, Swansea was the key centre of the copper-smelting industry.

The port of Swansea initially traded in wine, hides, wool, cloth and later in coal.

Brangwyn Hall is a multi-use venue and hosts a Festival of Music and the Arts. The city has three Grade One listed buildings namely Swansea Castle, the Tabernacle Chapel, Morriston and the Guildhall with its white Portland stone and a tall clock-tower which makes it a landmark. There are also a number of Grade II* listed buildings in the City.

The Victorian Grand Theatre celebrated its centenary in 1997.

Swansea City A.F.C. and the Ospreys Rugby Football Club is are based at the Liberty Stadium situated north of the City. St Helens Rugby and Cricket Ground is the home of Swansea RFC and Glamorgan County Cricket Club have previously played matches there. On this ground, Sir Garfield Sobers hit six sixes in one over; the first time this was achieved in a game of first-class cricket.

The Norwegian Church is a Grade II listed building in the docklands area of the city. built as a place of worship for Norwegian sailors when they visited the UK. It was relocated from Newport to Swansea in 1910. Swansea University has a campus in Singleton Park and opened a new Bay Campus situated in the Jersey Marine area of Swansea.

Other establishments for further and higher education in the city include University of Wales Trinity Saint David and Gower College Swansea.

Swansea Airport is a minor aerodrome situated on Gower providing recreational flights only.

The poet Dylan Thomas was born in the town and lived here for 23 years. His take on Swansea was that it was an "ugly lovely town". A bronze statue of Dylan Thomas stands in the Maritime Quarter.

Swansea Castle

The National Waterfront Museum is a museum forming part of the Museum Wales and deals with Wales' history of industrial revolution and innovation.

DAY 6   Swansea to Cardiff

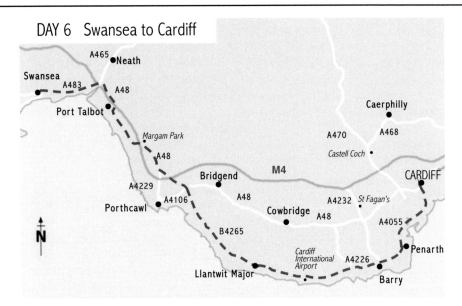

PORT TALBOT

is best known for its steelworks, one of the biggest in the world. The local beach, Aberafan Sands, is situated along the edge of the bay. In 1970 a new deep-water harbour was opened by Queen Elizabeth II and the Duke of Edinburgh.

Margam Country Park is situated about 2 miles from the town and within the park are three notable buildings: Margam Abbey, a Cistercian monastery; Margam Castle, a neo-Gothic country house and the 18th-century Orangery. The remains of a Chain Home Low early warning radar station, designed to guard against enemy surface craft and submarines in the Bristol Channel, are situated in the Park.

The estate is noted for its peacock population. Also on the estate are deer, first introduced by the Romans, Aviaries on the estate house a number of rescued birds of prey. The rare breed, Glamorgan cattle, are raised on the estate. A narrow gauge train conducts visitors around the grounds in the summer. Events on the estate are held through the summer ranging from fairs selling particular goods to car rallies. The Margam Country Show is held in August.

Access is free but there is a charge for car parking and for some events.

NEATH   A settlement since Romans times, it was a market town that expanded in the 18th century with the iron, steel and tinplate industries. Coal was mined extensively in the surrounding valleys and the construction of canals and railways made Neath a major transportation hub. The River Neath is a navigable estuary and Neath was a river port until recent times. The ruins of the Cistercian Neath Abbey, now in the care of Cadw, was once the largest abbey in Wales and substantial ruins can still be seen.

BRIDGEND

has greatly expanded in size since the early 1980s and is undergoing a redevelopment project, with the town centre mainly pedestrianised. Several prehistoric burial mounds have been found in the vicinity of Bridgend, suggesting that the area was settled before Roman times. A Roman road known locally as the 'Golden Mile' is believed to be where Roman soldiers were lined up to be paid. Three castles, Coity, Newcastle, and Ogmore provided a "defensive triangle" for the area.

COWBRIDGE

lies on the site of a Roman settlement and alongside a Roman road. The town centre is still arranged on its medieval plan, with one long street containing a number of Georgian houses. It is one of very few medieval walled towns in Wales, and substantial portions of the walls, together with the south gate, are still standing. The present Cowbridge Town Hall, served as a prison until 1830, when it was converted into a Town Hall. Eight of the original prison cells are still intact, six of which house the exhibits of Cowbridge Museum with the remainder of the building used by the town council and for public events. The Carnes' town house is a Grade 2* listed property of Medieval origin.
The town hosts the annual Cowbridge Food and Drink Festival which currently takes place in late spring. Many of the town's inns hold beer, ale and cider events.
The Cowbridge Music Festival takes place every autumn in various venues throughout the town.

LLANTWIT MAJOR

has been inhabited for over 3000 years and archaeological evidence shows that it was occupied in Neolithic times. It still retains its narrow winding streets, high walls, old town hall and gatehouse, and several inns and houses dated to the 16th century. In the beach area are the remains of an Iron Age fort.

BARRY

was a village with a port and its own church and watermill. It grew when it was developed as a coal port in the 1880s. The coal trade was growing faster than the facilities at Tiger Bay in Cardiff could handle so the docks at Barry were constructed and opened in 1889 to be followed by two other docks and extensive port installations. By 1913 Barry was the largest coal exporting port in the world. Whitehouse Cottage, the oldest existing inhabited house in modern Barry, dates from the late 1500s with the east end of the building added in around 1600. It overlooks the sea at Cold Knap.
Barry Island peninsula was an island until the 1880s when it was linked to the mainland as the town of

Barry expanded. Barry Island is now known for its beach and Barry Island Pleasure Park also the location of the popular TV series Gavin & Stacey.

PENARTH

area has a history of human inhabitation dating back at least 5000 years. Much later, streets of terraced houses with corner shops and public houses with local grey limestone were built giving a particular character to the town's older buildings. Penarth earned its wide reputation as "The Garden by the Sea" because of its attractive parks, open spaces and beach. A substantial part of the town has been designated as a Conservation Area because of its Victorian/Edwardian architecture. Penarth Pier, 750 feet long, was opened in 1895, and following damage caused by collision by ships the pier was rebuilt, strengthened, refurbished and revamped to be re-opened as a major tourist attraction in the Autumn of 2013.

CARDIFF

Most famously the buildings in Cathays Park, in the centre of the city are:-
1) City Hall. 2) National Museum of Wales.
3) Welsh National War Memorial. 4) University of Wales Registry Building all of which are built of Portland stone imported from Dorset.

Since the 1980s, Cardiff has seen major development and from 2000, there has been a significant change of scale of buildings both in the city centre and Cardiff Bay.

A new waterfront area at Cardiff Bay contains the Senedd building (home to the Welsh Assembly(5) opened on by The Queen in 2006) and the Wales Millennium Centre arts complex (6). This redevelopment in the Bay area has transformed it into an attractive, vibrant area.

Welsh Assembly building

Millennium Centre

Cardiff City Hall was opened in 1906 and built as part of the Cathays Park civic centre development and is an example of the Edwardian Baroque style.

The National Museum of Wales founded in1905: the museum has collections of archaeology, botany, fine and applied art, geology, and zoology. The art gallery houses a collection of Old Master paintings as well as other classical works.

Cardiff Barrage

Cardiff Bay with the Pierhead building and Millennium Centre in the background

The Welsh National War Memorial was unveiled in 1928 by the then Prince of Wales and commemorates the servicemen who died during the First World War and has a plaque for those who died during the Second World War.

Cardiff Castle is a medieval castle located in the city centre. The original motte and bailey castle was built in the late 11th Century by Norman invaders on top of a 3rd century Roman fort. Further work was carried out in the second half of the 13th Century.

Roath Park Lake
The clock tower at the southern end of the Lake commemorates Captain Scott's ill-fated expedition to the South Pole; his ship the Terra Nova sailed from Cardiff in 1920.

Cardiff University, founded in 1833, was originally in Newport Road where the Applied Sciences now stand, and is now in Cathays Park.

The Principality Stadium is the national stadium of Wales and is the home of the Wales national rugby union team. It has also held Wales national football team games as well as several other major events.

Pier Head is a rich terra cotta Grade One listed building. Built in the late 1800's as offices for the Bute Dock Company.

St FAGANS NATIONAL MUSEUM OF HISTORY

is one of world's leading open—air museums and Wales's most-visited heritage attraction. It showcases historic buildings relocated from across Wales, including a farm, a tannery, mills and a chapel.

LLANDAFF CATHEDRAL stands in the ancient city of Llandaff two miles north of Cardiff and dates from 1120. Throughout its history it has been altered, ruined and restored including the 15th Century bell tower & 19th Century Gothic architecture. Following war damage the interior was also repaired with an arch spanning the nave carrying Jacob Epstein's Aluminium Christ in Majesty.

CASTELL COCH

is a 19th-century Gothic Revival castle built above the village of Tongwynlais off the A470 north of Cardiff. The first castle on the site was built by the Normans after 1081 and the outside of the castle was rebuilt between 1875 and 1879.

Castell Coch's external features and the High Victorian interiors led it to be described as "one of the greatest Victorian triumphs of architectural composition." The surrounding beech woods contain rare plant species and unusual geological features and are protected as a Site of Special Scientific Interest.

CAERPHILLY CASTLE situated on the A469 some 8 miles north of Cardiff is the largest castle in Wales - second only to Windsor. Massive walls, towers and gatehouses were combined with sprawling water defences to cover a total of 30 acres. It was constructed in the second half of the 13th century and is famous for having introduced concentric castle defences to Britain and for its large gatehouses. It is thought that subsidence, when the water defences retreated, caused the southeast tower to lean outwards at an angle of 10 degrees as there is no evidence of deliberate destruction having been ordered. The castle is protected as a scheduled monument and as a Grade I listed building.

The following section details areas of interest adjacent or close to the Route namely:

Anglesey with its seascape, Snowdonia with its mountain scenery, South Pembrokeshire's stunning coastline and Gower Peninsula, Britain's first Area of Outstanding Natural Beauty.

Benllech Bay
Anglesey

Tryfan
Snowdonia

Dale
Pembrokeshire

Caswell Bay to Langland
Gower

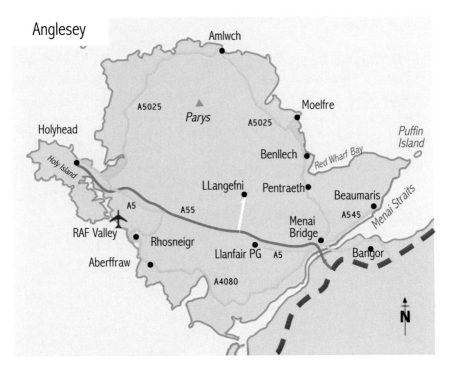

Anglesey

ANGLESEY has an area of 276 square miles and is by far the largest island in Wales with a population of some 70,000. Several small towns scattered around the island, make it evenly populated. It is a relatively low-lying island with the highest mountain, Holyhead Mountain, 220 metres.

There are numerous megalithic monuments and menhirs on the island. British Iron Age and Roman sites have been excavated and coins and ornaments discovered.

The rural coastline was designated an Area of Outstanding Natural Beauty in 1966. It has many sandy beaches, notably along its east coast between the towns of Beaumaris and Amlwch and the south west coast from Ynys Llanddwyn through Rhosneigr. The north coast has dramatic cliffs with small bays. The Anglesey Coastal Path around the island is 124 miles long and passes by/through 20 towns/villages.

The town of Amlwch was once largely industrialised with the important copper-mining industry at nearby Parys Mountain.

The Royal Air Force station - RAF Valley is home to the RAF Fast Jet Training School and Head Quarters of 22 Sqn Search and Rescue Helicopters, both units providing employment to about 500 civilians.

Tourism is now the major economic activity on the island. Agriculture provides the secondary source of income with local dairies being some of the most productive in the region.

Anglesey supports two of the UK's few remaining colonies of red squirrels. The RAF airstrip at Mona is a nesting site for skylarks. The sheer cliff faces at South Stack near Holyhead provide nesting sites for huge numbers of auks, including puffins, razorbills and guillemots, together with choughs and peregrine falcons. Anglesey is also home to several species of tern, including the roseate tern.

MENAI BRIDGE

designed by Thomas Telford and built by Robert Stephenson, the son of George Stephenson the famous locomotive engineer, opened in 1826 and provided the first road link between Anglesey and the mainland.

BEAUMARIS Castle was the last of the strongholds created by Edward1 in Wales. It is of near-perfect symmetry with four concentric rings of defence and included a water-filled moat and its own dock. A lack of money is believed to have resulted in its distinctive squat shape.

Puffin Island, just off the coast of Anglesey, is uninhabited and is designated a Site of Special Scientific Interest (SSSI) on account of its large cormorant population. Puffin Island has a breeding colony of some 40 Puffins, much less than Skomer Island off the Pembrokeshire coast. As well as the birds, there are grey seals on the island, and occasional sightings of bottlenose dolphins and harbour porpoise.
It is not possible for visitors to land on the island without permission from the landowner. However if you want to see the birds then the best way is to take a boat trip around the island from Beaumaris.

PENTRAETH

meaning, in Welsh, the end of or head of a beach was in 1170 the site of a battle when Hywel ab Owain Gwynedd landed with an army raised in Ireland in an attempt to claim a share of the kingdom of Gwynedd following the death of his father Owain Gwynedd. He was defeated and killed here by the forces of his half-brothers Dafydd ab Owain Gwynedd and Rhodri.

RED WHARF BAY is an Area of Outstanding Natural Beauty and close to Castell Mawr Rock, believed to be the site of an Iron Age fort.

BENLLECH

a popular beach holiday destination. The beach has an abundance of clean yellow sand and looks out toward the Great Orme. The village has a range of hotels, camping and caravan sites and several bed and breakfasts. The Scheduled Monument Pant-Y-Saer on the outskirts of Benllech is an enclosed "hut group" monument which consists of a complex of mainly circular huts and parts of an associated substantial enclosure wall lying on a slightly elevated limestone plateau area. The monument is of national importance for its potential to enhance our knowledge of prehistoric Romano British settlement.

AMLWCH

The most northerly town in Wales and according to legend developed in the Middle Ages on a site that had a harbour which was not visible from the sea and so helped to reduce the chance of Viking attacks.

With the nearby copper mine, the world's biggest, at the nearby Parys Mountain, Amlwch grew rapidly in the 18th Century and was the second largest town in Wales after Merthyr Tydfil. The harbour was also extended to accommodate the ships needed to transport the ore. In the 1970s, Amlwch had an offshore single point mooring Oil Terminal which was used to receive large oil tankers which were unsuitable for the Mersey. The terminal closed in 1990. Attractions in Amlwch include its restored port area, its watch tower, maritime and copper mining museums, St Eleth's Church (dates from 1800) and the reinforced concrete Catholic church Our Lady Star of the Sea and St Winefride, built in 1937.

HOLYHEAD

is a major Irish Sea port serving Ireland and the largest town in the Isle of Anglesey. Built on Holy Island, which is separated from Anglesey by the Cymyran Strait and originally connected to Anglesey via the Four Mile Bridge and now by the Stanley Embankment.

In the mid-19th century a larger causeway was built, known locally as "The Cobb". It now carries the A5, the railway line and the A55 North Wales Expressway which runs parallel to the Cobb on a modern causeway.

South Stack on Holy Island

ABERFFRAW & LLANDDWYN

Ynys Llanddwyn is a tidal island; it remains attached to the mainland at all but the highest tides and provides views of Snowdonia and the Llŷn Peninsula.

Before leaving Anglesey don't forget to visit the small village with the longest name in Wales - **Llanfairpwllgwyngyllgogerychwyrndrobwllllantysiliogogogoch** which translates to "Saint Mary's Church in the hollow of the white hazel near a rapid whirlpool and the Church of St. Tysilio of the red cave".

A second crossing of Menai Straits, Britannia bridge, to provide a direct rail link between London and the port of Holyhead was opened in 1850. In May 1970, the bridge was heavily damaged by fire. and the structure was subsequently rebuilt. The superstructure of the new bridge includes a lower rail deck and an upper one carrying the North Wales Expressway opened by HRH the Prince of Wales in 1980.

around wales

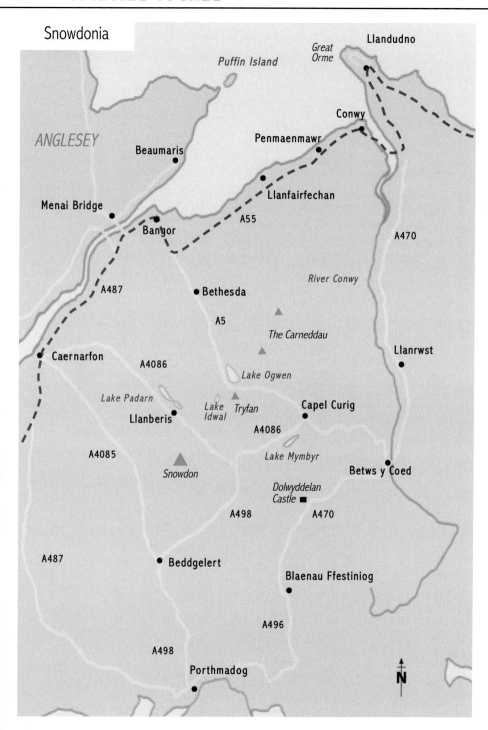

Snowdonia

Puffin Island

Great Orme

Llandudno

Conwy

ANGLESEY

Penmaenmawr

Beaumaris

Llanfairfechan

Menai Bridge

A55

Bangor

A470

A487

River Conwy

Bethesda

A5

The Carneddau

Caernarfon

A4086

Lake Ogwen

Llanrwst

Lake Padarn

Lake Idwal

Tryfan

Capel Curig

Llanberis

A4086

A4085

Lake Mymbyr

Snowdon

Betws y Coed

Dolwyddelan Castle ■

A498

A470

A487

Beddgelert

Blaenau Ffestiniog

A496

A498

Porthmadog

N

SNOWDONIA is the second-largest national park in Britain and contains a wide variety of other natural features - rivers, lakes, waterfalls, forests, moorlands, glacial valleys and a picturesque coastline. The area around Snowdon is the busiest part of the park popular for climbing and walking. Snowdonia was the area where members of the first successful attempt on Mt Everest trained.
Several of Wales' 'Great Little Railways' are found in Snowdonia.

BETHESDA

The town grew around the slate quarrying industries. Penrhyn Slate Quarry, Bethesda was once the largest and most productive slate quarry in the world and exported purple slate worldwide. The quarry men were suspended from ropes on the rock face and used explosives to remove large slabs of rock. The remains of inclined planes where rock was drawn up the galleries to the sheds or mills for slate processing is still evident. Part of the quarry, now modernised remains active, adjacent to the relict historic quarry. The system of benched galleries introduced here at the end of the 18th century/beginning of the 19th, is still evident along with the ropeway system (now used as an adventure zip-wire attraction and is the fastest zip wire in the world and the longest in Europe). The large tips of waste are a feature of the lower reaches of the Ogwen valley.

The narrow gauge Penrhyn Quarry Railway opened in 1801 to serve the Quarry connecting it with Port Penrhyn near Bangor and operated until 1962.
Bethesda has 40 Grade II listed buildings, including three pubs, in addition to the substantial and imposing Grade I listed Nonconformist Jerusalem Chapel.
Noted for its number of chapels the town was named after the Bethesda Chapel, built in 1823 and the town subsequently developed around it.

Lake Ogwen

CAPEL CURIG

is at the very heart of the Snowdonia National Park. A rugged mountain village and a mecca for climbing and walking in Snowdonia. Capel Curig is the home of Plas-y-Brenin — the national centre for mountain activities. As with much of the rest of the British Isles, Capel Curig experiences a temperate maritime climate but is one of the wettest places in the UK.

Betws y Coed

BETWS Y COED

A very popular inland resort where the River Conwy meets its three tributaries flowing from the West. Much of it was built in Victorian times and it is one of the principal villages of the Snowdonia National Park. Set in a beautiful valley in the Snowdonia Forest Park, it is ideal for outdoor activity holidays. Numerous Craft and outdoor activity shops are in the village with the popular Swallow Falls nearby. The main street has numerous inns and bed-and-breakfast accommodation.

A Museum with a miniature railway can be found at the railway station along with shops and restaurants.

The 14th century church of St Michael's is one of the oldest in Wales and is worth viewing.

Thomas Telford's iron Waterloo Bridge built in 1815, which carries the A5 across the River Conwy, bears the cast iron inscription "This arch was constructed in the same year the battle of Waterloo was fought"

DOLWYDDELAN CASTLE on the A470, a few miles west of Betws-y-Coed, in a spectacular setting, must be the most dramatically sited castles in Wales.

Along the A5 is Ty Hyll (The Ugly House), named because of the huge uneven boulders in its walls.

Slate quarrying in **FFESTINIOG** is actually slate mining worked on the underground principle of alternate openings and walls or supporting pillars of solid slate. In this they differ from the workings in Penrhyn and Llanberis which are of the open kind consisting of a series of terraced steps. The dip of the slate veins at Ffestiniog necessitates the winning of the slate by burrowing below the surface in order to follow the course of the slate-producing strata which are as much as 1,500 ft. or more down. A unique feature of Ffestiniog slate is its resilience,

which permits strips 1metre long or more, only 2mm. thick, being bent similar to a strip of steel. Apart from the manufacture of roofing slates, slate is widely used for billiard table beds, monumental purposes, brewery tanks, aquariums and pavements etc.

The slates were hauled by train on a narrow gauge railway laid in the early part of the 20th Century on a 2-ft. gauge track - at the time the pioneer of all narrow-gauge railways.

The National Slate Museum, LLanberis

DINORWIC QUARRY saw the first commercial attempts at slate mining in the late 18th Century. The business increased after the construction of a horse-drawn tramway to Port Dinorwic some years later. Towards the end of the 19th century when it was probably at its peak, some 100,000 tonnes was produced,

With the slate vein at Dinorwic being almost vertical and lying at or near the surface of the mountain, it allowed it to be worked in a series of galleries similar to that at the nearby Penrhyn quarry. The first quarrying was spread across some 16 sites and was a situation that lasted for many years.

The initial railway system brought transport problems as 5 quarries were all below the level of the railway and remained a problem for some 20 years when the lake level railway was built, the line of which is still evident today.

DINORWIG POWER STATION

The Dinorwig Power Station is a pumped-storage hydroelectric scheme, near Llanberis.
Construction began in 1974 and was completed 10 years later at a cost of £425m.
Dinorwig could store cheap energy produced at night by low marginal cost plant and then generate during times of peak demand, so displacing low efficiency plant during peak demand periods.
The scheme was constructed in the abandoned Dinorwic slate quarry. To preserve the natural beauty of Snowdonia National Park, the power station itself is located deep inside the Elidir Fawr mountain inside which there are tunnels and caverns. The power station is connected to the National Grid by underground cables to a local substation.
Water is stored at a high altitude at 636 metres in Marchlyn Mawr reservoir and is discharged through the turbines into Llyn Peris, over 500 metres lower, during times of peak electricity demand. It is pumped back up to Marchlyn Mawr during off-peak times. Although it uses more electricity to pump the water up than it generates on the way down, pumping is generally done at periods of low demand, when the energy is cheaper to consume.

The Snowdon Mountain Railway

Since 1896 visitors have been travelling to Llanberis, to experience this unique rail journey to the Summit of the highest mountain in Wales and England. Snowdon Mountain Railway has been described as one of the most wonderful railway journeys in the world with stunning scenery and awe-inspiring views.

BEDDGELERT

Once a busy port when the river was tidal and ships
sailed all the way to the village centre before the building of "the Cob" by the coast.

Beddgelert (the grave of Gelert) village owes its fame
to the story of Prince Llewelyn ap Iorwerth who decided
on a hunting trip and left his infant son in the charge of
his faithful dog Gelert. On his return, the Prince was
greeted by Gelert, who noticed the dog's muzzle was
soaked in blood, and his son nowhere to be seen.

Llewelyn attacked the dog, and it fell to the ground gravely injured. However, he heard a cry from nearby bushes
and found his son, safe in his cradle. Beside the cradle lay the body of a giant wolf covered with wounds, the result of a fight to the death with Gelert. It is thought that this story was made up by local traders some time ago

in an attempt to lure Snowdon's visitors to their village! The
tomb of Gelert supposedly stands in a beautiful meadow and
consists of a slab lying on its side, and two upright stones.
Experience the working environment of the Victorian miner in
the Sygun Copper Mine on the outskirts of the village.

For one of the most scenic drives in the whole of Snowdonia, take the A498 which follows the course of the
Glaslyn north-eastwards past two idyllic lakes - Llyn Dinas and Llyn Gwynant - before climbing up the Nant
Gwynant Pass into the rocky heights of Snowdonia.

Lake Idwal

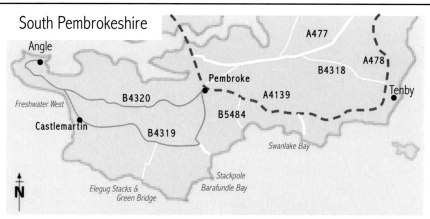

South Pembrokeshire

Some of Pembrokeshire's Beauty Coastal Spots

Stackpole Quay

Barafundle Bay

Freshwater West Beach

Swanlake Bay Beach

Elegug Stacks

Green Bridge

PLEASE NOTE the access road to Elegug Stacks and Green Bridge crosses MOD land and may be closed during Firing. Normal Firing Times are 09.00 - 16.30 for Day Firing: 18.30 - 23.30 for Night Firing. Check with the National Park on **0845 3457275** beforehand.

Gower Peninsula

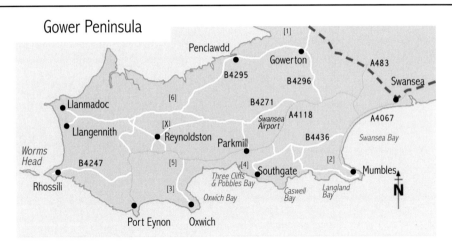

The Gower peninsula -

Britain's first Area of Outstanding Natural Beauty is known for its coastline, popular with walkers and surfers. The southern coast consists of a series of small, rocky or sandy bays as well as larger beaches such as Port Eynon, Rhossili and Oxwich Bay. The north of the peninsula is home to the cockle-beds of Penclawdd. The interior is mainly farmland and common land. The Peninsula has many caves, including Paviland Cave and Minchin Hole Cave and has been the scene of several important archaeological discoveries. In 1823, archaeologists discovered a fairly complete Upper Paleolithic human male skeleton in Paviland Cave. This was the first human fossil to have been found anywhere in the world, and is still the oldest ceremonial burial anywhere in Western Europe. Gower is also home to standing stones from the Bronze Age. Of the nine stones eight remain today. One of the most notable of the stones is Arthur's stone [X] near Cefn Bryn. This was most likely caried by glacial ice from some distance away.

Castles on the Gower peninsula include:

Loughor Castle [1], Oystermouth Castle [2[, Oxwich Castle [3], Pennard Castle [4], Penrice Castle [5] and Weobley Castle [6].

Arthur's Stone

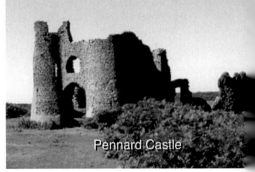

Pennard Castle

Rhossili Bay

Mumbles Lighthouse

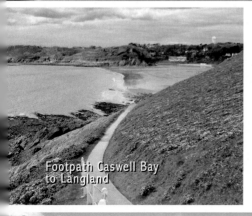

Footpath Caswell Bay to Langland

Pobbles & Three Cliffs Bay

Langland Bay

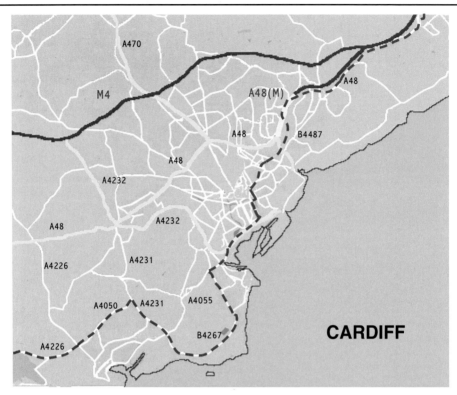

Some buildings of interest in the City

1. Welsh Assembly Building (Y Senedd)
2. Wales Millennium Centre
3. City Hall
4. National Museum of Wales
5. Welsh National War Museum
6. Cardiff University
7. Pier Head Building
8. Cardiff Castle
9. Roath Park Lake Tower
10. Principality Stadium
11. Cardiff Barage

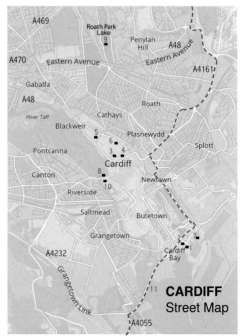

CARDIFF
Street Map

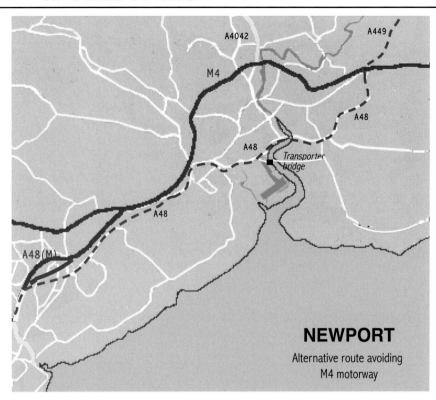

NEWPORT

Alternative route avoiding
M4 motorway

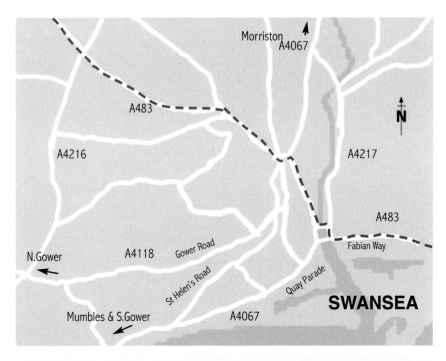

SWANSEA

NOTES

NOTES

INDEX